COME EAT WITH ME

COME EAT WITH ME

ROB DOUGLAS

RESOURCE *Publications* • Eugene, Oregon

COME EAT WITH ME

Copyright © 2018 Rob Douglas. All rights reserved. Except for brief quotations in critical publications or reviews, no part of this book may be reproduced in any manner without prior written permission from the publisher. Write: Permissions, Wipf and Stock Publishers, 199 W. 8th Ave., Suite 3, Eugene, OR 97401.

Resource Publications
An Imprint of Wipf and Stock Publishers
199 W. 8th Ave., Suite 3
Eugene, OR 97401

www.wipfandstock.com

PAPERBACK ISBN: 978-1-5326-7136-4
HARDCOVER ISBN: 978-1-5326-7137-1
EBOOK ISBN: 978-1-5326-7138-8

Manufactured in the U.S.A.   11/20/18

Scripture taken from the Holy Bible, NEW INTERNATIONAL VERSION®, NIV® Copyright © 1973, 1978, 1984, 2011 by Biblica, Inc.® Used by permission. All rights reserved worldwide.

Contents

Introduction: You are Invited | vii

Invitation to a Garden | 1

Finding Annie | 6

Guests with a Gift | 11

Stepping Forward, Stepping Back | 15

Hosting When You Can't | 20

Local Boy Made Good | 25

The Meal that Initiated Freedom | 30

A Town Built on a Sandhill | 34

Manna and Quail | 38

A Light in the Darkness | 42

A Place to Host the Maker | 46

A Pristine Destination | 50

Invitation to a New Land | 54

The Richest of Fare | 58

Come and Taste the Wine | 62

Who is This Man? | 66

An Invitation Up a Tree | 70

A Third Culture | 74

The Story of the Great Banquet | 78

Messy Hospitality | 82

The Expanding Lunchbox | 86

The Birdwatcher and The Cross | 89

Not Quite the Last Banquet | 93

The Meal that Unites | 97

A Stranger on the Road | 101

A Place of Healing | 105

Breakfast on the Beach | 112

A Bowl of Rice | 116

The Dream That Changed the World | 121

The Water of Life | 125

The Final Banquet | 129

In the Presence of My Enemies | 133

Bibliography | 137

Introduction

You are Invited

IN THIS BOOK I would like to invite you to come and eat with me. Like the host of a dinner party, I have prepared a night out for you with some good company, good food, and good conversation. And as your host, I would like to share some of the things I have learned about what it means to be part of the community of people who call themselves followers of Jesus. There are many ways this community, usually called the church, can be described, but in this book I want us to hear the invitation of God to come and eat with Him.

Over time, my wife and I have become devotees of cruising and have enjoyed cruises to various parts of the world. Our favourite cruise company, Princess Cruises, has registered the words "consummate host" they are so convinced about the high level of service that they offer to their guests. I hope the people at Princess don't mind me using those words in this book, but I've also read restaurant reviews that use a similar term. You see, I've come to realise that God is the consummate host, and, incidentally the ultimate guest, and as we learn from him, the community of his followers must learn the art of both hosting and guesting for themselves.

One of the places where relationship is encouraged the most is at a meal table. When young lovers go on a date, they will have a meal together. When people marry, they have a meal together and with their friends and family. Families find out about the events of the day and learn to value each other at a meal, and friends often have a meal when they simply want to get together. To invite someone to your table is important in developing relationships and creating intimacy. So when God invites us to his table, he is not just calling us to simply eat, but to enter into a relationship.

The invitation to eat is not just a metaphor for a relationship with God, but is a deliberate act required by anyone who becomes a follower of Jesus. Throughout both the Old and New Testaments of the Bible we are introduced to examples of people providing hospitality to others, along with direct instructions about welcoming strangers and providing spaces where people can grow and develop.

This book takes you through the Bible from beginning to end, telling a smorgasbord of stories that highlight God's role as a God of hospitality. As you read these stories my hope is that you will meet the consummate host, you'll accept the invitation to his table and you will enter into a thriving relationship with Him. As this happens you may also become aware that hospitality is something that is central to the Christian faith. Maybe you already call yourself a follower of Jesus, but have never thought of your relationship with God in this way. I hope that you will find something in this book that helps you grow in your relationship with the consummate host and will better understand the responsibilities that come with sitting at His table.

I also hope that the re-telling of stories from the Bible will ignite your desire to read the Bible and investigate this amazing book further. Christine Pohl, in her book *Making Room: Recovering Hospitality as a Christian Tradition* speaks about the importance of telling stories, and in many ways, she describes one of the goals of this book.

> We nurture hospitality as a habit and a disposition by telling stories about it. We retell the Bible stories of guests who turned out to be angels. We remember the stories of

You are Invited

Jesus' life – how he welcomed all sorts of people, how he fed thousands on a hillside, how he made breakfast for his friends. In our practice of hospitality, we also develop our own tradition of stories - mixtures of miracle, hard work, disappointments, and very funny encounters. We tell stories of real sacrifice and surprising blessing.[1]

I have written this book to help those who are considering the Christian faith, to dig deeper and discover what it means to be a follower of Jesus. To those who are already followers of Jesus this book is an invitation to think about your faith in a different way and to appreciate afresh the beauty of your relationship with the consummate host. It may also prompt you to begin conversations you never had before, about God's invitation and the responsibilities that come from accepting that invitation.

So pull up a chair to my table, and as you eat with me, I hope you will experience God in a fresh way.

Rob Douglas.

---

1. Pohl. *Making Room.* 1950

Invitation to a Garden

How God the Maker, the consummate host, prepared the table immaculately for his first guests.

THIS PLACE THEY CALLED Eden was all they had ever known and they loved it. This was where they belonged and they enjoyed exploring the many different nooks and crannies that opened up to them as they wandered through the hills, along the river, and through the juniper forest. They also enjoyed the regular chats they had with Maker as he came to the garden from time to time. They were never quite sure how he would appear next; sometimes he would come in the form of a lion, sometimes as a lamb. They enjoyed the surprise.

It was a perfect day as the man and the woman strolled hand in hand along the riverbank. The sun was warm on their backs and a light breeze gently kissed the leaves on the trees that grew prolifically along the river. In the distance they saw some gazelle grazing quietly on the lush grass. Then they were distracted by a closer movement, and they watched, fascinated, as a dragonfly hovered over the river before landing gently on a lily pad.

He had given them both various jobs to do. One was to give names to the animals and they delighted in watching tiny insects, creeping lizards and lumbering marsupials as they fed and interacted with each other, then tried to come up with names that in some way reflected their uniqueness. Maker called them Adam and Eve and they liked their names. Experimenting with language and how words could be used to describe their environment, then turning those words into names, was great fun. They wanted to come up with a name for him; he was a bit coy about telling them his name. They figured Maker would do for now.

On those days when he came to walk with them, Adam and Eve loved to hear stories of how their world came into being. They had a deep sense that he was the consummate host who had prepared this place for them with intricate detail, then graciously invited them to make it their own, naming the animals, caring for the vegetation, and creating a home for themselves. They enjoyed being with him and respected him and his wisdom. They even accepted, at first, his instruction not to eat the fruit of just one tree that was laden with delicious looking fruit. There was no shortage of amazing fruit on hundreds of other trees so there was no need to eat of that one forbidden tree. Initially, it seemed to make sense that there should be some boundaries, but as time went on they couldn't help but notice the tree and wonder how the fruit would taste.

During their evening walks, Maker told them about the time when there was nothingness and how he began to plan a beautiful place he could enjoy with his creation. They had begun to measure the periods of time the sun was shining, and appreciated the time of darkness so they could sleep. It seemed that somehow this rhythm made a lot of sense, but Maker told them during one of their chats that the sun wasn't the original source of light; that he had invented the idea of light and darkness even before he created the sun and the nighttime lights that watched over them as they slept. The division between land and water—the way the river ran through their garden and the dew watered the plants at night— all seemed so natural, but Maker told them that he had the idea of separating land and water even before he made the oceans and the rivers.

He told them about the way he had developed an amazing cycle of life in all kinds of vegetation: trees of all varieties; tiny plants creeping along the ground; shrubs and flowering plants.

They were maintained because they produced fruit and seeds that would become food for the next part of his creation, but would also fall to the ground, sometimes blown along by the wind to find new places where they would find opportunity to regenerate. They even noticed that animals would eat seeds that passed through their bodies and weeks later would sprout some distance from their host plant.

Maker got very excited when he talked about creating the snapper and barramundi, the storks, eagles and robins, then the cows, hedgehogs and lizards and he smiled as the man and woman told him the names they had given to these creatures as he described them. Adam and Eve were honored when Maker asked them to name the animals and to look after the environment because it was as if he had handed over a very special possession to their stewardship. They were not just visitors to Maker's country, but were honored guests who had been invited to make this their home and to take responsibility for everything he had made. Everything that had gone before was a preparation for them and for their descendants. It was as if the host was handing over the role of host to them.

The excitement in Maker's voice was unmistakable when he told Adam and Eve again and again about making them the peak of his creative activity. He had them in mind as he developed the idea of light and darkness and separated land and water. He thought about how people would benefit from the establishment of lights in the sky that linked with the changes between light and darkness, the provision of food and the means of building a home. He had a sparkle in his eye as he planned the excitement of livelihood that would fill the earth through vegetation and fauna, and become a living, dynamic home for his people. He thought about the provision of meaningful activity and most of all he thought about the relationship that would develop between him and these people whom he had made with such enjoyment.

The sun had gone down behind the horizon and the stars were twinkling in the dark dome that hovered above. Adam and Eve lay back on the grass and tried to count the stars. Maker had prepared all this for them and they were overwhelmed at the level of detail. Nothing was out of place.

"What was snake doing over by the big tree earlier today?" Adam asked, still gazing up at the stars.

"He was talking about that tree. Said the fruit was pretty good," Eve responded. "We can trust him, can't we?"

"Dunno," Adam mumbled. "There's something about him that worries me, but I must admit that fruit looks beautiful."

"You're not wrong— But Maker did say not to eat the fruit off that tree. Snake said he'd be back again tomorrow. Perhaps we can have another chat with him then."

As the two lay on their backs looking at the stars, for the first time they felt uneasy about looking at each other. It seemed that something new had entered their perfect world. Something they couldn't describe. For the first time they were glad of the darkness because it seemed to provide some sort of privacy from feelings they had never experienced. And for the first time they hoped they wouldn't bump into Maker on his evening stroll through the garden.

They lay silently for a while then Eve asked: "Why did Maker put that tree there if we're not allowed to eat from it?"

It was the first time the question had been verbalized, but Adam acknowledged that the thought had crossed his mind on more than one occasion.

"Everything's just right," he said. "Maker wouldn't have put the tree there if it wasn't right for it to be there. Giving us a choice must also be right."

"So, being able to make a choice is part of Maker's perfect plan?" Eve asked. Then before Adam could reply, she added: "And snake's part of his plan too?"

For a long time they lay silently staring at the stars. The consummate host had thought of everything. He had provided them with this beautiful place, he had invited them to participate with

INVITATION TO A GARDEN

him in looking after his creation, he had given them responsibilities and authority... and it was now dawning on them he had given them the ability to decide between good and evil.

You can read the story for yourself in Genesis chapter 1 and 2.

Finding Annie

I'VE BEEN TO A lot of conferences in my time but few keynote speakers were as memorable as Anne McDonald. Using an alphabet board to communicate, Anne brought to her audience an awareness of how far an understanding of disability had come within our own lifetime.

As I sat with hundreds of other people listening to this diminutive woman in a wheelchair speak about her life experiences, it was hard to appreciate that just over twenty years earlier, Anne had commenced legal action to seek permission to be released from an institution in which she had lived for eighteen years.

Anne McDonald's experiences were the subject of the 1984 Australian movie, Annie's Coming Out which was based on a book Anne wrote some years earlier with Rosemary Crossley. Anne was only three years old and had been diagnosed with severe cerebral palsy when her parents placed her in an institution for people classified with severe disability. For the next eleven years Anne lived there without education or therapy, suffering neglect and starvation. When Rosemary Crossley, a therapist, met Anne she weighed only twelve kilograms and appeared to have no communication capacity, but Rosemary sensed that while she had a physical disability it did not mean she was intellectually impaired. Over the years Rosemary worked with Anne until she completed her university entrance exams, then a humanities degree before becoming a popular conference speaker and author.

Finding Annie

When I started working in the disability sector in 2000, I was unaware of the huge changes that had occurred in disability support in just a few years. I began meeting regularly with a few parents of children with disabilities, and quickly learned that stories like Anne McDonald's were not unusual. In fact, the transition from institutional care was still continuing. It was an even greater shock to me to learn that these parents had never been invited to consider what sort of life their children would choose if they were given the opportunity.

Sure enough their children were home with them, rather than in an institution which would have been the case if they had been around twenty years earlier, but their support was still governed by an institutional-type of thinking. Various wonderful not-for-profit organizations were funded to support individuals but in most cases individuals had to fit in with whatever program was on offer at the time. The parents I met with argued that the choice of going bowling on Thursday night wasn't a choice at all. Nor was it acceptable that their children were bundled into a bus with a whole lot of other children with disabilities to be taken on an outing to a park, while children without a disability could ride their bikes, go to the beach and play with their choice of friends.

These conversations enabled me to link with other people who were having similar conversations and to become part of a movement that led to the establishment of services based on individualized funding and opportunities for individuals to make creative decisions about their own lives. People with disabilities were able to live in their own homes with a live-in carer, they could attend mainline schools instead of "special" schools, they could go on to study at university and find employment in the open workforce. All of this in the same lifetime that people had been forced to live in institutions and considered hopeless cases because of the nature of their disability.

But as I exercised my mind about the way in which we provided services to people with disabilities I began to think about another institution. I have been involved with the church for most of my life and in that time, I have seen some bad examples of a self-serving self-maintaining institution, and I have also seen the church as a community that builds people into better people.

The premise of this book is that God has invited us to come and eat with him, and to discover what that might look and feel like. Let's continue this journey through the Bible and get a sense of what it means to eat at God's table. I suspect right from the beginning that it's got little to do with establishing an institution.

I want us to discover what a Christian community could look like if we were to follow the images that are provided in the Bible and to do that without being too influenced by our preconceptions of the church and what it has looked like in the past. But that doesn't mean the process is going to be without some difficulties. In fact the challenges were there right from the very beginning.

The Bible starts with a great picture of God preparing the table, placing the first people in a garden where everything is beautiful. But within a short time, they have come across a challenge. They are given a choice about eating some fruit from a single tree, and the suggestion that is put into their minds by the snake is that eating of the fruit will give them knowledge about the difference between good and evil.

Prior to that, everything was good and life was pretty simple. I think we'd all like that kind of life, and joining God's community on earth would be pretty cozy if we didn't have to worry about choices between good and evil. But the choice the first people made had immediate consequences, and it was their own family that suffered from their decision.

It's interesting that the story about the sons of the first people involved a meal. Abel was a sheep farmer and was very proud of the way he cared for his flock and was able to develop exciting new methods of animal husbandry. His brother Cain was a farmer and he was equally proud of his ability to grow crops that would produce delicious food.

I can imagine the day Cain harvested one of his early crops, and successfully developed the process of baking a loaf of bread. He invited Abel to kill a sheep, and together, with all their families, gathered in great excitement to eat a meal together. What a time of celebration that would have been. But perhaps the happy families weren't as happy as it seemed on the surface.

Cain, it would seem, was jealous of his brother. Perhaps it was because the family liked the roast lamb and found the bread a little dry without any butter and jam which, by the way, hadn't yet been invented. Certainly, the decision of Cain's parents to explore the idea of understanding good and evil was starting to work its way into Cain's psyche.

In recognition of God and as an expression of thanks to him Cain and Abel each brought a portion of their produce and made an offering to God. But there was a problem. We're only into the fourth chapter of the Bible and we're told that God who has invited us to come and eat with him rejects Cain's offering, and in a jealous rage, Cain kills his brother.

Why did God reject Cain's offering? It wasn't anything to do with the quality of his produce, but more to do with what was lurking in Cain's heart. As we work our way through this book we will make an exciting discovery. The evil that was crouching at the door of Cain's heart prompting him towards jealousy and then murder, was to follow humanity for the rest of time. When Cain brought his gift of grain to God, it was not done in a spirit of thanksgiving and love, but, I would suggest, was a process of institutionalizing the act of worship. The act of bringing an offering wasn't a genuine response from the heart, but the act of someone who was doing what they thought needed to be done.

Why did God reject Cain's offering? Hold that question for a while, because the vast story of the Bible is all about the answer to that question. Over time we will discover in the stories about God's invitation to eat with him, that the evil that lies deep within will continue to disrupt many potentially beautiful meals, but in the long run a solution is at hand.

Anne McDonald lived in an institution for eleven years where people believed she was a vegetable with no hope of living any sort of life outside of the institution. But one day Rosemary Crossley took her to an art gallery and saw something in her eyes that prompted her to question this popular belief. She then spent the rest of Anne's short life discovering the vibrant person who was trapped inside a seemingly lifeless body.

In his invitation to us to eat with him God isn't inviting us to an institutionalized meal, but to join him in a relational community where we can hear his voice of acceptance, and see the spark of life in the eyes of another. In fact, the whole story of the Bible is about his invitation and our place at that banquet.

Guests with a Gift

How God the Maker, the consummate host, visited some people one day, not as host, but as a guest, and almost in camouflage, provided an amazing gift to his hosts.

It was a sweltering hot day and Sarah was thankful for the shade of the great oak trees under which Abraham had pitched their tent. She had hooked up a tent flap to allow any breeze to blow through but in the middle of the day there was no breeze and the only respite from the searing heat was to lie quietly and wait until the evening before attempting any work.

Despite the heat and the perspiration dripping down her forehead into her eyes Sarah was close to sleep when a noise prompted her to pull herself up onto her elbow. Abraham had been sitting at the door of the tent taking advantage of the shade from the oak trees. He was a good man. He was nearly 100 years old and had been a faithful husband. It was harder to get around these days and although she was a few years younger than Abraham, Sarah was feeling her age as well. There was only one thing that had been a note of sadness in their long life together. Abraham and Sarah had no children.

Sarah could see Abraham slowly pulling himself up onto his feet and she peered out of the darkness of the tent into the dazzling sunshine to see what had prompted him to move away from the shade. She could hear a voice and wondered who would be visiting their tent in the heat of the day, so moved a little closer to the door of the tent to get a better view of what was happening outside. Abraham was moving away from the tent and she could see what looked like three figures standing in the shade of the oak trees.

She made sure that no-one would be able to see her, but was anxious to get into a position where she could see what was happening and hopefully overhear the conversation. Visitors were rare, so she was anxious to find out who would be travelling through the hot desert sun to come to visit them. As she peered through a crack in the walls of the tent she sensed there was something intriguing about the three figures under the oak trees.

Now Abraham was moving quickly towards the strangers and Sarah watched as he bowed low to them. Abraham obviously didn't know who these visitors were, but she smiled to herself because the way in which he bowed before them was typical of his gracious approach to all people, particularly strangers. He was only with them a few minutes, then began making his way back to the tent. Sarah slipped back to where she had been lying so it wouldn't be too obvious she had been watching what was going on.

Abraham leaned over and stepped into the tent. "Quick," he said, "get three seahs of the finest flour and knead it and bake some bread. I'm going to get a calf and kill it for these visitors. Oh, and get them some curds and milk as well." Sarah quickly got up and began preparing the bread as Abraham headed out of the tent at a rate that Sarah found a little disconcerting considering the heat of the day.

"Take it easy," she called out to Abraham as he disappeared into the harsh sunlight.

While she was waiting for the bread to bake, Sarah edged back to her place near the door of the tent where she could remain unseen, but could watch what was going on. Abraham had found a place under the oak trees for the visitors to sit and was ably fulfilling the role of host to these strangers. Fortunately, they were just within earshot, so although Sarah couldn't catch everything that was being said, she could hear just enough to keep her glued to her position.

"Where is your wife Sarah?" they asked Abraham.

Sarah was taken aback: "Who were these men? How did they know my name," she thought to herself.

Abraham was answering them now: "She's just there, in the tent." Sarah quickly pulled back away from the door of the tent just in case they looked up and saw her. She tried to stay within earshot because she didn't want to miss anything now.

The one in the middle was an imposing figure, though there was something distinctive about all three of the men. There was something that made them stand out from the traders who came by their tent from time to time. They certainly didn't look like locals, but she couldn't place where they might have come from.

The one in the middle then said: "I will surely return to you about this time next year, and Sarah your wife will have a son."

Sarah nearly blew her cover as she gasped. She pushed her shawl over her mouth to cover the sound of her laughing. Who was this man? Who did he think he was? She was well past childbearing years and although Abraham often talked about how sad he was that he didn't have children, she knew that it wasn't going to happen.

She tried to compose herself and was glad that the bread had finished baking and she was able to take it out to the visitors. It may give her a chance to see them a little closer. But as she approached them, one of the men asked Abraham why Sarah had laughed when he said that she would have a son. It was an embarrassing moment. Abraham looked flustered, unsure how to answer the question, so Sarah piped up. "Oh, I didn't laugh," she lied. But the man looked directly at her and said, "yes, you did laugh."

At that moment Sarah knew that these were no ordinary men. She had a sense that this was God himself, the three in one, who could not only predict the future, but knew what was happening in the darkness of the tent, and more significantly, in the secret places of her mind.

Come Eat With Me

As the men stood to leave, the one in the middle said: "Shall I hide from Abraham what I am about to do? Abraham will surely become a great and powerful nation, and all nations on earth will be blessed through him. For I have chosen him, so that he will direct his children and his household after him to keep the way of the Lord by doing what is right and just, so that the Lord will bring about for Abraham what he has promised him."

Abraham and Sarah looked at each other as the men disappeared into the distance. "Did you hear what they said," Abraham stammered. "They were no ordinary visitors. We have just been visited by the Lord Almighty. I have hosted the Lord and he has eaten my bread and meat.

Sarah looked up at Abraham. "And as you provided for him, he has provided for us. Our guest has provided a great gift."

You can read the story for yourself in Genesis chapter 18

Stepping Forward, Stepping Back

I'M NOT IN THE habit of organizing dinner parties, but if I were there are some things I would consider. To start with the decision to hold a dinner party is not usually made in isolation. There's usually a reason, perhaps a birthday or some other celebration, and there are some people I would want to join me in that celebration. I would then start to prepare for the event. That would involve setting the date, organizing the venue, planning the food, the entertainment and the decor, and organizing invitations. As time got closer I would be thinking carefully about where people should be sitting, who would sit next to whom, and perhaps what people shouldn't be sitting together. I may get some other people to help me in this process of preparation, but as host I would be stepping forward to make sure that everything was just right.

On the night of the dinner party I would be at the door welcoming people in and making sure they were introduced to people they didn't know, that they felt comfortable and safe in a place they may not have visited previously. From that point on I would probably step back and participate in the party. If I had done the right amount of preparation the evening should proceed without too much input from me. In fact, I would have no control over the nature of the conversations that would ensue, the relationships that may develop, or how people would perceive the food, the entertainment and the company.

I had created a space where a group of people could come together and magic might happen, but that magic would not be my doing. During the night I may step back to take a wider view of the room to ensure that everything is going well and take notice if anyone didn't seem to be fitting in. I may retreat to the kitchen to make sure the details are in order, and if I see people sitting alone, I may try to initiate conversation and connections. I'll also join in along with all the other guests, eating, drinking and holding conversation.

As the host I would not be the focus of the dinner party, but my role would be critical in ensuring that each individual could find their own place on the night, and that great connections would occur. By stepping forward when it was necessary and stepping back at just the right time an opportunity would be provided for individual guests to shine, for great stories to be told, for food and wine to be enjoyed, for new relationships to be formed, for old relationships to be revived, and for the guests to go home at the end of the night with great memories.

Mark McKergow and Helen Bailey in their 2014 book, *Host*, introduce hosting as a new metaphor for leadership, and show how a leader, in the role of host, steps both forward and back in their responsibilities. The real art, they say, is in knowing when to do what. There are times when it's necessary for the host to take responsibility for certain situations and tasks, but there are other times when it is important the host can disappear into the background and allow people to participate as equals. They talk about times when the host needs to be in the kitchen, at other times eating with the other guests, and sometimes standing back in the hallway getting an overall picture of what is going on.

They describe six roles of engagement for the host leader, as an initiator, an inviter, space creator, gatekeeper, connector and co-participator. Initiators respond to the world around them and get things going. As an inviter, a host leader thinks invitationally. It's about reaching out and engaging with people in a way that "invites rather than insists." A space creator creates spaces in which events can emerge and unfold. McKergow and Bailey recognize a dichotomy between active planning and what they call emergent responding. While a gatekeeper is usually seen as someone who excludes others, the authors argue that a host leader who acts as a gatekeeper is concerned with drawing boundaries that create and sustain progress. Connectors build connections between people, link people and ideas, and know when to leave them to get on with it. Co-participators not only prepare for their guests and plan appropriately, but they also join with their guests in the experience.

McKergow and Bailey contend that the traditional idea of leadership seems to suggest a focus on the leader, but by using the metaphor of host it is much easier to focus on the idea of leading as a relationship between the leader and others.

> "Having drawn people together, a good host won't dominate the situation. He/she will flit from one section to another, with a word here and a touch there, keeping an all-encompassing eye on how things are going. But the host won't hog the limelight or become tiresome by constantly taking centre stage. The host is always on the lookout for when to intervene and when to leave things ticking along – when to step forward and when to step back. The role of the host transcends and includes both. It entails awareness and timing – and acting instantly."[1]

The images of God throughout the Bible provide a picture of someone who is indeed the consummate host; someone who takes center stage one moment, then at another time steps back, even to the point of becoming the guest at times. Yet through all that, he maintains his place as the one who we can always look up to as our leader. As we look to his leadership we learn what it means for the community of his followers to follow his example and to exist in harmony with him and with each other.

The idea of hospitality as a spiritual principle was discussed forty years earlier by author and priest Henri Nouwen in his book *Reaching Out: The Three Movements of the Spiritual Life*. Nouwen addresses the question: "What does it mean to live a life in the Spirit of Jesus Christ?" He argues for three movements in the spiritual life: from loneliness to solitude; from hostility to hospitality; from illusion to prayer.

---

1. McKergow and Bailey, *Host* Kindle locations 242–244

He describes hospitality as a rich Biblical term that can deepen and broaden our insight in our relationships to our fellow human beings. "Old and New Testament stories not only show how serious our obligation is to welcome the stranger in our home, but they also tell us that guests are carrying precious gifts with them, which they are eager to reveal to a receptive host."

Nouwen says that when hostility is converted into hospitality, fearful strangers can become guests revealing to their hosts the promise they are carrying with them.

> "Then, in fact, the distinction between host and guest proves to be artificial and evaporates in the recognition of the new found unity. Thus the biblical stories help us to realize not just that hospitality is an important virtue, but even more, that in the context of hospitality guest and host can reveal their most precious gifts and bring new life to each other." [2]

Another goal of this book is to show that the art of hosting is embedded in Scripture from beginning to end and hospitality is part of the character of God. I have re-told Bible stories and interspersed them through the book as a way of discovering something about the way in which hospitality comes from the heart of God and has become an aspect of the life of the Christian community. By drawing on this understanding we can begin to learn about what it means to be a community and how to live in relationship with God.

When God created the world, he was preparing a place for the human beings who would represent the peak of his creative process. Adam and Eve had the privilege of living in this amazing world that was created for them, enjoying the presence of the host walking and talking with them, and appreciating the various responsibilities he gave to them. As the host of that beautiful garden he passed on hosting responsibilities to Adam and Eve that included making decisions that would have eternal significance. They were safe within that beautiful place and they were not there

---

2. Nouwen, *Reaching Out.* 47

by force, but by invitation. They had the choice of staying and enjoying that place in communion with their host, or taking the way out and isolating themselves from their host. They chose the latter.

As time went on, another ordinary human being by the name of Abraham was singled out by God as a leader for his people, but the moment when he was granted the promise that would make all his potential come to fruition was a time when Abraham became host to his God. Under the oak trees of Mamre, Abraham met three men, possibly a picture of the God who is three-in-one, Father, Son and Holy Spirit, who promised Abraham he would become the father of a great nation. Rather than God hosting Abraham in a special celebration, the promise occurred in an environment where Abraham was the host and the heavenly visitors were guests. The gracious God not only acts as host, but steps back from time to time to receive hospitality from his guests. He continues to do this each time the Christian community gathers to worship and to serve him as their honored guest.

The idea of God becoming a guest rather than host is repeated through the Bible and highlights this concept of "stepping forward, stepping back." God doesn't deal with us in some kind of power play, and the relationship between us and God should never be institutionalized to give the impression that he is not approachable. There are images of God in the Bible that create in us a sense of awe and reverence, and his holiness and transcendence are important to our acceptance of a spiritual being that is beyond our comprehension. The uniqueness of his character is that when we least expect it, we find him stepping into our world as a very ordinary human being.

The story of a poor widow who became host to a prophet illustrates how those who reflect God's character are granted the capacity to humble themselves and become like a servant.

Hosting When You Can't

How God the Maker, the consummate host provided grace to enable someone to become a host when it seemed impossible.

THE COUNTRYSIDE AROUND ZAREPHATH where Naomi lived was dry. A terrible drought had fallen on the land; the grapevines had stopped producing, and even the majestic olive trees were dying. Food sources had dried up and the economy of the country was in disarray.

Naomi was near the gates of her home town of Zarephath in Lebanon where she was looking for sticks that may have been left lying on the roadside. Her young son's gaunt face never left the mind of this poor widow as she desperately looked for enough pieces of wood to take home to make a fire. She had enough flour to make some bread, but needed a fire to bake the bread and it was even harder to find firewood in these desperate times.

As Naomi bent down to pick up a few sticks off the road she spotted a man on the road that led into the town gates from the countryside. He was obviously a traveler. His feet were dirty; his hair disheveled. She stood up. There was something about this man that distracted her from her task but before she had time to hide her obvious interest, she realized he was heading towards her.

As he approached he called out: "Would you bring me a little water in a jar so I may have a drink?" Naomi knew what it was like

Hosting When You Can't

to be thirsty and hungry so was quite willing to get a drink of water for him, but, as she turned to head towards the well, he called, "And please bring me a piece of bread."

Well, that annoyed her a bit. Surely he could see that she was collecting firewood and wouldn't be in a position to feed a stranger. Her reply was terse. "Can't you see? I don't have any bread. I've got a handful of flour at home and a little olive oil in a jug but I'm gathering a few sticks to take home and make a meal for myself and my son. Once we've eaten that, we'll probably die."

Naomi picked up the bundle of sticks she had left on the side of the road, ready to leave the stranger to find his own support. She turned towards home, but before she could take another step her intentions melted at the next words she heard.

"Don't be afraid," the stranger was saying. "Go home and do as you have said. But first make a small loaf of bread for me from what you have and bring it to me, and then make something for yourself and your son. For this is what the Lord, the God of Israel, says: 'The jar of flour will not be used up and the jug of oil will not run dry until the day the Lord sends rain on the land.'"

All sorts of thoughts were swirling through Naomi's head as she listened to these words. She was angry at his impertinence but there was something about him that, against all her better judgement, seemed to ring true.

Who was this man who had appeared out of the blue and was asking Naomi for water and bread? What did he mean when he said the jar of flour will not be used up and the jug of oil will not run dry until the day the Lord sends rain on the land?

Begrudgingly, she invited the man to follow her to her home so she could give him something to eat and drink. As they walked, Naomi discovered his name was Elijah and that he called himself a prophet of the Lord. She was a little suspicious of someone describing themselves in such a way but she listened as he told her that he had recently been to see King Ahab. Naomi had heard all the reports about King Ahab and the evil that he perpetrated over the years. She had heard the little groups of people in the marketplace grumbling about his leadership style and his rejection of the ways of God. Elijah's story seemed to fit with what she had heard about the king, but she wasn't expecting the next part of the story.

Naomi's son greeted them at the door as they arrived at her house and she ushered Elijah inside and invited to sit down while she bustled around the kitchen trying to find some food for him. All the time he kept talking. It seems he had turned up at the king's office without an appointment but had been able to get in to him and announce that there wouldn't be any dew or rain over the next few years without his word. Elijah explained to Naomi that this was a message from the Lord as a way of helping Ahab to become aware that God was in control of the elements.

The more Elijah talked the more Naomi began to realize that everything he said was true and she was, in fact, hosting someone with significant spiritual credentials. It was rather amazing to her that Elijah had predicted the drought on the land, but here he was feeling the effects of it himself. Despite being a prophet of the Lord, he wasn't immune from the outcome of his own words. As she became more and more convinced, Naomi decided to offer Elijah her spare room and to share the small jar of flour and the jar of oil with her and her son until it ran out.

Days and weeks went by and Naomi and her son had gotten used to having Elijah around the house. She had been the perfect host and had made Elijah feel welcome in her home. He knew that Naomi and her son were suffering as a result of the climate change he had predicted to the king, yet she seemed to graciously continue with her life without complaining. Each morning she got up and looked in her cupboard at the jar of oil and the jar of flour. Each morning she expected to see them empty but there was always something left. Naomi quietly closed the cupboard door and breathed a prayer of thanks knowing that God was providing for her needs.

Sadly the day came when her son who had been quite ill over a period of time, passed away. Naturally she was angry, sad and frightened all at once. A great mixture of emotions filled her heart as she confronted Elijah and said, "What do you have against me, man of God? Did you come to remind me of my sin and kill my son?"

Elijah heard her angry outburst but he didn't react to it except to quietly go into the boy's tiny bedroom where he wept before the Lord in prayer. Naomi had been so good to him over a difficult period in his life, but the drought had been particularly harsh on Naomi and her son. As he wept before the Lord, the tears falling on the face of the cold body in front of him, he thought about the punishment that God had meted out of the evil king, and the way in which Naomi and her precious son had suffered in some kind of collateral damage.

Elijah was tempted to blame himself as he thought about the situation that Naomi now found herself in, and as he cried before the Lord he reminded his God of the way Naomi had taken a stranger into her home, had fed him and provided him with a comfortable bed. He thanked God for the way in which the jar of flour and the jar of oil had never run out in all the time Naomi had hosted his stranger. And as he leaned over the boy and wept before the Lord he felt a movement. Elijah wiped the tears out of his eyes and looked at the boy. His chest heaved and he coughed, then slowly his eyes opened and he looked up at Elijah.

Naomi had been sitting at the kitchen table, her head in her hands, but a noise prompted her to look up. She gasped. Elijah was coming into the room carrying her son.

"He just needs a good feed," Elijah joked as he put the young man down on the chair in front of his mother. Naomi gasped, then threw her arms around the boy who was sitting upright on the chair, rubbing his eyes.

"Now I know that everything you said is true," she said through tears of joy.

"Your gift of hospitality to a hungry stranger was a great blessing," Elijah said but before he could add anything else Naomi held up her hand to stop him.

Come Eat With Me

"The jar of flour and the jar of oil that never ran dry, and now this... my son is alive... I have received far more than anything I gave. My jar is overflowing with grace from Almighty God."

You can read the story for yourself at First Kings chapter 17.

Local Boy Made Good

As I look back over my life I sometimes wonder how things all worked out, but I've come to the place where I have to acknowledge that God had a plan that was bigger than anything I could have imagined. During my high school years, we were told we needed to talk to the guidance officer about our plans for the future so that an appropriate course of studies could be planned out into senior high school.

I had no idea what I wanted to do, but when a careers expo was held at the school, my dad and I trotted along to see if anything would spark my interest. We looked at the board at the front of the school and I saw the heading "communication," so headed off to where the manager of the local radio station was manning a stall. A week or two later I went in for my meeting with the guidance officer and when he asked me what I wanted to do when I left school, I told him I wanted to be a radio announcer. Apparently, that was not a sensible career choice, and he told me so.

When I left school, I began investigating radio announcing, but when a job was advertised in the local newspaper, I applied, and was successful. This job, reading copy and marking it up ready for the sub-editor led to me doing a cadetship, and finally being formally graded as a journalist.

At the age of twenty-five I left journalism to attend theological college, and assumed that I had given up journalism for good to take up a life in Christian ministry. However, within a few years of graduating I took up a position as a bi-vocational pastor in a remote town in the far north of the state of Western Australia. The tiny new church was only able to pay me the basics, so I fell back onto my trade of journalism, among other things, to make a living.

Another fifteen years working in three remote communities as a bi-vocational pastor saw me taking on many diverse jobs including hospital cleaner, supermarket shelf-packer, education coordinator at a local prison, community services manager, marketing consultant in the tourism industry and surprisingly, founding editor for a new community newspaper. Having thought I had put journalism behind me to pursue service for God, God returned my gift to me and allowed me to use it for his service.

In time, another experience came my way as an executive manager in the community services industry where I gained valuable management experience in the areas of disability, mental health, counselling and aged care. Then, after a seven-year break from pastoring I found myself, for the first time, as a full-time pastor of a local church. Perhaps, when the word communication sparked my interest at that high school careers expo it was actually the Holy Spirit popping a word into my mind that was to carry me through the rest of my life.

The story in the Bible of a young boy by the name of Joseph is another reminder of the way God intervenes in people's lives to bring about his purposes.

Joseph was unlucky in a way. He was born when his father was old, so by the time he was a teenager his ten older brothers had well and truly labelled him as "daddy's favorite." The fact that his dad had some special clothes made for him didn't help, but what made it worse was that Joseph didn't fit the family mold. The older brothers were men's men. They were hard workers who liked the rough and tumble life of sheep farming, and found it hard to accept Joseph's more refined ways.

They were prepared to stay out in the paddocks for long periods of time and teased him every time he excused himself from their late nights of telling dirty jokes around the campfire, to go home to Dad. They suspected that he didn't have too many good things to tell their dad about what was going on in the workplace.

Local Boy Made Good

The fancy clothes his dad gave Joseph riled them, not just because it seemed their dad was favoring their little brother, but because he would even dare to turn up at work looking like he was too good to get his hands dirty.

To make matters worse, Joseph was a dreamer. Not just a day dreamer, but he literally had dreams about himself and his brothers, and in every dream, things turned out well for him, and not so good for his brothers. But instead of keeping the dreams to himself, he told his brothers about them, including the bits that highlighted his own achievements.

To cut a long story short, Joseph's brothers took the rather cruel action one day of kidnapping Joseph and selling him to some traders who took him to far away Egypt. Things went pretty bad for Joseph initially but in time, he found his feet and worked his way through government bureaucracies to take a leading role in the country, at a time when famine was destroying the livelihoods of people far and wide.

In an effort to obtain food Joseph's father, who thought Joseph was dead by now, sent his sons to Egypt because he had heard that there was an emergency relief program that had been established by a high ranking official. He had no idea the official was Joseph, and when the brothers arrived they didn't recognize him, dressed as he was in the garb of an Egyptian official. Joseph, the annoying little brother, was to become the consummate host to his brothers, providing food to them at a time when they and their families were threatened with starvation.

Joseph led them on for a while, but in time identified himself, resulting in the whole family, including his younger brother Benjamin, and his parents, experiencing an emotional reunion. He was able to organize food and housing for the family, and because of his position of influence made it possible for the whole family, along with their families and friends, to move from Canaan to Egypt where they settled and established a strong community of expatriates.

Over a period of 430 years the Hebrew community lived in Egypt and grew in number and influence. Although they began as refugees, they quickly integrated into Egyptian society and participated in every level of community life. Within a generation, the original circumstances of their arrival were forgotten, and these people with different cultural and religious practices, were taking over Egyptian jobs. Threatened by the growing power of a race that was now integrated into every aspect of Egyptian society, authorities began to introduce oppression as a way of maintaining their own strength. Whether it was the Hebrews who built the pyramids in Egypt can't be confirmed, but in time they were turned into slaves in an effort to limit their growing power.

It was during this time that another Hebrew leader emerged by the name of Moses. It fell to Moses, a young man with little experience in leadership, to convince Egypt's pharaoh to release the Hebrew people from slavery. Like a trade union leader, Moses faced the difficult task of emancipating a permanent workforce who were central to a nation's economy, and leading them back to Canaan, the original homeland of their ancestor Joseph.

I've taken the time to explain how the Hebrew people became slaves in Egypt because the next part of the story is essential to our understanding of how God prepared his table. Just as the Hebrew people originally came to Egypt in search of food, a meal was to become the final act of emancipation.

This meal was called the Passover and it marked the end of an era for the Hebrew people as they completed their time in Egypt, but also marked the beginning of a new phase in the life of a nation. While it was a significant event on its own, it also became an important memorial for the Jews for millennia to come. Each year families would come together to eat the Passover and remember that event when they were freed from slavery in Egypt.

In time, Jesus introduced something new to the Passover, replacing the Passover lamb with his own body. John the Baptist, who announced the coming of Jesus, described Jesus as the Lamb of God who takes away the sin of the world (John 1:29), and one of Jesus's followers, Peter, also described him in terminology that reflected the Passover lamb.

> For you know that it was not with perishable things such as silver or gold that you were redeemed from the empty way of life handed down to you from your ancestors, but with the precious blood of Christ, a lamb without blemish or defect. He was chosen before the creation of the world, but was revealed in these last times for your sake (First Peter 1:18–20)

As God prepared the table for his people, a meal was provided that became a turning point in history and set the scene for the future. It was a meal that wasn't without pain, but was infused with hope and purpose.

The Meal that Initiated Freedom

How God the Maker, the consummate host, initiated a meal that was to represent the emancipation of a whole community.

Freida was feeling quite anxious about the events of the last few days. There had been rumors all over town that something big was going to happen and now Father had come home from an urgent meeting and had called an unexpected family gathering. Life wasn't always easy for the family of twelve-year-old Freida, but she had never seen her father so stressed. He was quite secretive about the purpose of the meeting, but spoke with an urgency in his voice that wasn't normal for a man who usually seemed to take life so calmly.

As the family crammed into their tiny front room, Freida looked around wondering what father was about to say. Mother had an anxious look on her face, but was busy trying to keep the baby quiet, while trying to stop two-year-old Golda from trying to climb on to the back of a goat that was nosing its way in the door. Freida's oldest brother Reuben took over the task of rescuing the goat from Golda's grasp, then pushed the inquisitive animal outside where it belonged. She was very proud of Reuben who was now a teenager and was taking on many of the jobs that once were the responsibility of his father.

The Meal that Initiated Freedom

Eventually silence fell over the room, apart from the occasional whimpering from the baby. Father began to explain the meeting he had been to with Moses, a man who had emerged as a leader among the Hebrew people in recent months. It turned out Moses had been in many high-level meetings with the Egyptian pharaoh and, in line with the rumors, had been influential in creating a great deal of fear in the minds of the Egyptian hierarchy, as well as the general populace. There had been a number of plagues in recent times that had mainly impacted the Egyptian people and from the whispered conversations Frieda had heard between her mother and father, there was a high level of anxiety in the community.

The news that Moses had delivered to the Hebrew men he had called together that morning was a shock to everyone. As father explained what Moses had told them at the meeting, his voice began to tremble. There had been little evidence of the plagues on the eastern delta of the Nile where the Hebrew community lived but for some of the Egyptian cities their effect had been devastating. Over time the Pharaoh had been worn down and Moses had told the gathered men that the previous evening he had met with Pharaoh and delivered an ultimatum that he had received from God.

Freida had never seen her father so emotional as he pulled Reuben to his side and put his arm around his shoulder. "Later this month an angel of the Lord will come across the land of Egypt and the eldest son of every household will die," he stammered. A single gasp seemed to come from every mouth around the room, and mother let out a shriek. "Wait," said father. "We've been given some very detailed instructions about what we have to do."

The family moved in a little closer so they wouldn't miss a word. "On the tenth day of the month, each Hebrew household is to take a one-year-old male lamb and look after it carefully for the next four days." Father began to explain details about the lamb, and what was to happen after that, but Freida wasn't following. Her mind wandered as she looked around the room, particularly watching Reuben to see how he would react to what his father was saying.

The details didn't bother Freida, but she knew that Reuben and his father would have the instructions very clear, and she and mother and the rest of the family would do whatever they were told to do. Sure enough, as soon as the meeting was over mother called Freida to her and began to explain what she needed to do to prepare for what was clearly a very significant event. Following the instructions to the letter would not only ensure the safety of her beloved brother Reuben, but was critical to the future of her people.

Over the next few days Freida took more notice of what was about to happen. Apparently, they were to prepare a meal of the lamb and to eat it, along with unleavened bread. The blood was to be splashed on the doorposts, and during the night their family would be joining the other families in their community in a desperate dash to escape Egypt while the Egyptian families were grieving the sudden loss of their eldest sons.

During a break in preparations, Freida took a walk down by the river to catch up with her friends, Ruth and Rhoda. They had all received the same news from their fathers and were both excited and afraid about what was to happen. As the girls sat on the riverbank they shared their thoughts about the meal that they were told would be called a Passover.

"This is all very exciting," Freida said. "Father says that if we follow the regulations exactly, eat the meal in just the way we have been told, and put the blood on the doorposts and the lintel, then we'll be able to escape from Egypt."

"That'll be great," Ruth said quietly. "Every night my father comes home in pain. He tries to hide it from me, but I've seen mother dabbing his back with a cloth. Apparently, they have to move great blocks of stone and are beaten if they don't work fast enough."

"I know. My father's the same," the other two girls added in unison.

"I've heard father screaming at night because of the pain," Rhoda said. "I don't even have a chance to ask him about it in the morning because he's gone off to work before breakfast. Mother won't say anything, but I've seen her crying.

"God knows all about the pain we're experiencing," Freida said. "Father says that God has asked us to prepare this meal as a way of showing that we trust him and are prepared to be obedient to him. We will be set free from slavery if we are prepared to show that we believe in God and will follow his instructions.

"I think we've got some work to do, girls," she added as she jumped to her feet. "Let's go and help get ready. We can't leave this to father and mother, this is something for the whole family. I'll race you to the corner. Come on!"

A Town Built on a Sandhill

WE WERE STANDING ON the side of gently sloping sandhill about as far away from anywhere as you could imagine. As far as our eyes could see, low scrub covered the landscape, interrupted only by the occasional stand of stunted tree and the undulating shape of red sandhills. There was no sign of human habitation within sight and certainly no indication that this sparse bushland would one day host a bustling community.

I was with the manager of a new iron ore mine that was being established in the north eastern goldfields region of Western Australia about 1000km northwest of the capital city of Perth and a two hour drive from the nearest town. As a journalist I had been following the construction of the mine and had been invited to inspect the site of a proposed town that would service the mine and become home to about 700 workers and their families.

The mine manager proudly kicked some stones raising a small cloud of red dust and waved his hand up the sandhill. "This is where I'm going to live," he said. As we walked over the sandhill, we had the advantage of inspecting a set of plans for the proposed town and were able to imagine how this isolated piece of bushland may one day look.

About forty years later I visited the township of Leinster, now showing the signs of decades of existence as a rough and tumble mining town. It was an experience that few people can share, and it was hard to imagine what the location once looked like without houses, shops and roads. An arid sandhill was now a place where people lived and worked, ate and slept, played and did business. What I had once seen as a set of architect's drawings was now a town that had its own history, and had created its own set of memories.

When the Hebrew people made their way through the isolated and lonely countryside between Egypt and what had become known to them as the promised land, there were no permanent towns established, but a strong community took shape. One event after another helped build a network among the travelers, but also established a connection with God as their travel guide and leader.

There in the wilderness they learned to trust in God and began to learn what it meant to be a godly community.

In the mid-20th century Mrs L.B.Cowman wrote a daily devotional which has become a Christian classic, called *Streams in the Desert*. In it she helped her readers appreciate that God provided the sustenance required to cope with the hardships of life. For forty years the Hebrews travelled towards what they hoped would be a new world, and in that time a nation was established.

> "All our supply is to come from the Lord. Here are springs that shall never dry; here are fountains and streams that shall never be cut off. Here, anxious one, is the gracious pledge of the heavenly Father. If He be the source of our mercies they can never fail us. No heat, no drought, can parch that river, 'the streams whereof make glad the city of God'.

> "The land is a land of hills and valleys. It is not all smooth nor all downhill. If life were all one dead level of dull sameness it would oppress us; we want the hills and valleys. The hills collect the rain for a hundred fruitful valleys. Ah, so it is with us! It is the hill difficulty that drives us to the throne of grace and bring down the shower of blessing; the hills, the bleak hills of life that we wonder at and perhaps grumble at, bring down showers. How many have perished in the wilderness, buried under its golden sands, who would have lived and throne in the hill country; how many would have been killed by the frost, blighted with winds, swept desolate of tree and

fruit but for the hill—stern, hard, rugged, so steep to climb. God's hills are a gracious protection for His people against the foes!"[1]

Cavan Brown was a pastor who proceeded me by some decades in a pastoral ministry in the remote northwest of Western Australia. *Pilgrim Through This Barren Land* was a book Brown wrote as a result of his experiences in the desert and his observation that the desert experience was a critical aspect in the growth and development of the Hebrew community, and subsequently the life of those who became followers of Jesus.

> "The importance of these forty desert years needs to be appreciated in the light of Israel's impact on history. The faith that was formulated in the desert became the foundation for three major faiths in the world - Judaism, Christianity and Islam. It was a faith that survived and outlived the combined might of the Egyptians, Assyrians, Babylonians, Persians and the Roman empire. It surpassed the influence of the Greek philosophers and superseded numerous religious systems based on confusion, superstition and unrelenting fear.
>
> "While the faith discovered in this period has had some sad aberrations in history, the truth remains that the emergent principles of this forty-year period have done more to raise the dignity of humanity and the quality of life than any other period in human history. Even Jesus Christ made no attempt to depose it—he said he came to fulfil the Law and not replace it. This momentous piece of history began in relative obscurity—with a nondescript tribe who claimed to have met God in a remote location with a fierce desert landscape." [2]

Brown went on to talk about a meal that God provided in the desert for the Hebrew people as they travelled. The provision of manna, a bread-like substance, and quail, sustained the people

---

1. Cowman, L.B., Streams in the Desert
2. Brown. *Pilgrim Through This Barren Land.* 113

for much of their journey and represented a turning-point in their relationship with God.

> "The manna was more than food; it brought the people of Israel into a relationship of complete dependence on God. It spoke to them of a direct and immediate relationship between God and his gifts. It was also given to them alongside the gift of the word (message) of God and a union was established between man's physical and spiritual needs; between manna and the word of God. They learnt that wholesome human life can only be sustained when manna and word are seen as coherent requirements that are provided by God in a recognized direct and immediate relationship. The desert environment is seen as crucial in the learning of this lesson."[3]

The Hebrews were treated as slaves in Egypt, but they had gotten so used to the life that the stability of their existence had become familiar and safe. Their journey through the wilderness threw up many challenges, but in that they were slowly being drawn together in a nation-building exercise. Perhaps not surprisingly, their journey began with a meal, but shortly along the road, they were invited by God, once again, to eat with him, and this time to meet their gracious host in a new way.

From tiny beginnings on a scrubby sandhill, I had the privilege of seeing a thriving community grow and develop, and there was a sense of satisfaction in being able to sit in a coffee shop and look around me at the township that had grown over many years. I wonder what God was thinking as he looked on the Hebrew people and saw their sense of community, wellbeing and belonging develop on their journey through the desert, and the way in which the people ate at the tables he set, and in the process a nation was formed.

---

3. Brown. *Pilgrim Through This Barren Land.* 148

Manna and Quail

How God the Maker, the consummate host, provided a unique meal but set some important boundaries that would enable the growth of a lasting relationship.

IT WAS JUST A month since that hurried Passover meal in Egypt, and Freida was struggling to get her head around everything that had happened in that time. They had eaten the meal and without time to say goodbye to her friends, the family had thrown as many of their belongings as they were able on to a cart and headed off in the direction of the Sinai Peninsula. Having said that, Freida was sure her friends were doing the same thing, but there were so many people pouring out of the houses and rushing down the streets, it was hard to tell who was a part of this mass exodus, and who might have planned to stay.

Some people were pulling handcarts, some people had carts hitched up to their animals. Children ran back and forth among the crowds, while anxious parents tried to keep them in check and make sure they didn't get lost in the crush. Over the next weeks Freida had found her friends and family groups were travelling together, sharing stories as they went.

Although they had brought some food with them they now found themselves struggling to find enough to eat. People were starting to grumble about why they were even carrying out this strange journey. They had been caught up in the excitement of the

Manna and Quail

moment, and now it seemed the holiday was over and it was time to go back home where there was a level of stability, even if life wasn't perfect. Then something unexpected had happened.

Frieda and her best friends Ruth and Rhoda were excitedly talking about the strange events of the last few days as they made their way past the campsite to a place where they could have some quiet from the crying babies.

"It was getting really horrible, the way everyone was complaining," Frieda said.

"Yes, my dad was even saying that we would have been better off staying in Egypt, than coming out here," Ruth prompted.

"You should have heard my big sister and her friends," Rhoda added. "They were going on about the great food we used to have in Egypt. I think they'd forgotten what it was really like." But can you believe what happened?

The girls stopped walking and looked at each other as they went over the events that had occurred a week earlier. Moses had told the people that God was going to provide food for them and sure enough that evening, as they were sitting outside their tents, they spotted quail walking and fluttering through the camp.

"I thought there were just a couple of birds," Frieda said. "Then I realized they were everywhere. There were a couple of quail having a sand bath just near the opening of the tent and father grabbed them."

"I know." Rhoda laughed. "Did you see the way people were chasing after them. The boys thought it was great fun."

"But they tasted great," Ruth mused. "I was really hungry, and I helped mum cook them. I nearly started eating before they were cooked properly, but mother said, no we're going to make a really nice meal out of this.

"But by the time we had finished dinner, they had all gone," Frieda said. "Then at dusk the next night they were there again, and it's been like that every evening."

"God has been good," Rhoda added. Moses told us that God had heard our prayer and had promised that he would meet our needs.

"But what about the manna?" Freida asked.

"Yes, that was weird," the other two girls said together.

"I woke up that first day and there was dew all over the ground," Freida said. I got out of my tent to have a look, and as the sun came up the dew disappeared and the ground was covered with this stuff."

"It was like frost, wasn't it?"

"I thought it was a bit like the color of coriander seed," Ruth added. Mum came and woke me up to have a look. I've never seen anything like it."

"But what about the taste?"

"It was kind of, like a wafer, but made out of honey," said Rhoda. "Hard to describe."

People had started to call this bread-like substance manna, and it appeared on the ground around their campsite every morning. The instruction Moses had given the people was that they were to collect as much as they needed for their family, just for that day. He also added that on the day before the Sabbath they were to collect extra so they would have enough for the next day.

As could be expected there was always someone who wanted to push the boundaries, and sure enough some people had collected some extra quail so they would have quail meat for breakfast. The next morning they had woken up and discovered there were maggots in the meat. The same thing had happened with the manna, by the time the sun came up properly the manna just seemed to melt away, and it was a waste of time even trying to keep extra.

Some people tried to test the boundaries about the Sabbath requirements as well. The idea about observing a sabbath rest day wasn't yet in their consciousness. This was something completely new to them, and they weren't quite sure of its purpose. Moses explained to them that on the seventh day they were to take a break from their normal duties and dedicate the day to God, who even provided double the amount of food on the previous day, so they wouldn't have to go out collecting food on the sabbath rest day.

Moses explained the process very clearly, but sure enough, on the sabbath day there were some people out foraging around

Manna and Quail

the campsite trying to find manna. They figured they didn't need to collect extra the previous day as they had been told, but just as Moses said, they couldn't find any and they found themselves unable to feed their family.

"Why do you think we have these rules about the sabbath rest day?" Freida asked absent-mindedly.

It was nearly sunset when the quail would be coming out. The girls pondered Freida's rhetorical question for a while, then Ruth spoke quietly.

"Maybe the gift of the quail meat and the delicious honey manna wasn't just about meeting our needs. Maybe it was about us helping to appreciate and value God. That's why he's asked us to put aside a special day; to remember that love goes both ways."

The girls got up and began to run back to their tents. They didn't want to miss their evening quail hunt.

You can read the story for yourself at Exodus chapter 16

A Light in the Darkness

THE GOLD RUSH OF the 1890s was an important time in the history of Western Australia with people coming from all over the world in search of the precious metal. As prospectors arrived pushing wooden wheelbarrows that carried a pick and shovel, a tent and a few belongings, small communities began to develop. In time, towns were established with hotels, banks and town halls being erected out of stone and brick, while houses and other temporary structures were often built out of wood and corrugated iron. In what had previously been rugged bushland, dozens of small towns became home to the hundreds of gold-seekers, along with those who sought to make their fortune out of the success of the gold-seekers.

Today there is little evidence of these thriving communities, some of which have disappeared altogether. In some cases all that is left of these "ghost towns" is a pile of bricks and some trees that differ from the surrounding landscape, perhaps a reminder of a time when a lonely publican's wife tried to produce a garden to ease the harshness of her environment. In most cases the surrounding bushland has taken over what were once streets, backyards and shops.

My assignment as a young journalist was to find a prospector by the name of Jasper Bright who was the last inhabitant of one of these nearly forgotten ghost towns in the isolated north eastern Goldfields. I arrived at Kookynie late in the afternoon after a long drive and found, to my surprise, a lonely hotel, still open to quench the thirst of prospectors and pastoralists in the surrounding area. In an effort to retain the memories of the past, a local family had resolutely kept the business going despite the hardships of isolation and economic pressures. In 1900, the Grand Hotel was one of six hotels in a busy community. I asked the way to Jasper Bright's house and was directed down a bush track which 100 years before would have been a busy thoroughfare for all types of fortune-seekers.

The sun was going down when I got to the ramshackle corrugated iron shack that had been Jasper's home for as long as this ghost town could remember. He welcomed me in and offered me a cup of black tea in a tin mug. As we sat and talked about days gone by in Kookynie, I became increasingly aware that the room was lit by a single hurricane lamp. As far as I could see there was no electricity to provide what I would have called the necessities of life. As the sun disappeared the lamp appeared brighter and the faint orange glow it produced filled the darkened corners of the room.

When the Hebrew people left Egypt on their journey to the Promised Land they were guided by a pillar of cloud in the daytime and a pillar of fire at night. These were symbols to the people that God was with them and was leading them. Jasper Bright's lamp may have put out a small amount of light, but its presence became more evident as the sun disappeared, in the same way that pillar of fire would have provided assurance of the presence of God.

Over time it became obvious that without a clear focus, their journey was likely to become an aimless activity that would lead them nowhere, and that internal squabbles would eventually lead to self-destruction. As their leader, Moses became a spokesman for God and passed on a range of laws, instructions and guidelines to help them in their daily life as a nation-in-formation. Surprisingly, a total of thirteen chapters, a fairly large slab of writing in the early pages of the Old Testament, are filled with Moses' instructions about building a mobile place of worship, called a tabernacle.

The instructions about how the tabernacle would be built and what it would look like were very detailed and the casual reader could be left wondering why on earth so much time is spent writing about what was essentially an up-market marquee. The point of it all, however, was that this structure that could be pulled down and erected in another location as the people travelled, was to represent the presence of God with his people. Wherever they went and whatever circumstances they faced, the existence of the tabernacle was a constant reminder that God, who had led them out of slavery in Egypt, was always present.

When they finally settled in the Promised Land decades later, a more permanent structure, a temple, was built by King Solomon that continued to be a focal point for the worship of God. An awareness of the presence of God had evolved from the faint light of a pillar of cloud of fire in the night sky, to a portable place of worship and then to the construction of a massive stone building that was never intended to move. But that wasn't the end of the story.

When we proceed to the New Testament we find Paul writing to the church in Corinth and making an astounding statement: "For we are the temple of the living God. As God has said, 'I will live with them and walk among them, and I will be their God, and they will be my people.'" The pillar of cloud and pillar of fire were to prepare the people for the portable tabernacle, which prepared them for the more permanent temple, and all of these were symbolic of what was yet to come: The real temple was to be the people of God.

At the death of Jesus, the curtain of the temple was torn in two from the top to the bottom. Prior to that nobody could access the most holy place without receiving the services of a duly accredited holy person. With the curtain ripped in two, the people were being told in a symbolic fashion that God was accessible to all. What they didn't realize at the time was that the whole approach to God's presence was changing. God's presence with his people was no longer to be represented by cloud or fire, nor by a building, either temporary or permanent.

> Consequently, you are no longer foreigners and strangers, but fellow citizens with God's people and also members of his household, built on the foundation of the apostles

and prophets, with Christ Jesus himself as the chief cornerstone. In him the whole building is joined together and rises to become a holy temple in the Lord. And in him you too are being built together to become a dwelling in which God lives by his Spirit (Ephesians 2:19–22).

The astounding result of this is that if we are prepared to sit at God's table we become the presence of God to those around us. In that place we are fully representing his characteristics and his grace to whoever is willing to sit with him. Just as people who walked into the camp saw the tabernacle and recognized that God was present in that place, so the presence of God becomes obvious through his people who are willing to sit and eat with him.

A Place to Host the Maker

How God the Maker, the consummate host, initiated the construction of a portable place of worship that would act as a symbol of his presence in the community.

ELDAD CONSIDERED HIMSELF TO be a fairly proficient carpenter, but he had never seen a set of plans like the one that had just been delivered to him. His job was to build a table that would be located in what everyone was referring to as a tabernacle. Moses, their leader, had delivered instructions that a portable place of worship was to be constructed, and every tradesman, needle-worker, and craftsperson was mobilised to the task.

The table was to be built of acacia wood which was good because Eldad noticed that this was the main source of wood throughout their travels so far. Fortunately, some of the younger men had been organised to access the best trees and provide him with sufficient timber for the job. He enjoyed working with acacia, but he also knew that it was a highly durable timber and its water-resistant quality meant that it made a handy piece of furniture. Not surprisingly, Eldad may not have been aware at the time that acacia was naturally anti-bacterial so was ideal for serving food.

The table that Eldad was commissioned to build would be a focal point within the tabernacle. It was one of a number of pieces of furniture that were to be strategically placed within the structure. In his mind, Eldad pictured where the table would be situated and where it would be placed in conjunction with the rest of the furniture. He also listened to how other tradesmen were describing their plans and imagined the timber frames that were to be erected and the elaborate system of curtains that would line the whole structure. Ultimately the tabernacle could be taken apart to enable them to move camp, then expertly re-erected at the next camping site.

The instructions provided to Eldad required the table to be nearly a meter long, half a meter wide and about 60cm tall, which he observed, was not a particularly large table. He had been told that when it was finished it was to be overlaid with pure gold, with a gold molding around the rim. With that information he could have been tempted not to worry too much about the final standard of his workmanship, because nobody would get to see his joints or the grain of the timber, but Eldad had a sense that this was to be a job that required his best work.

As he planed the wood to a beautiful smooth finish Eldad reflected on the importance of his task. Being a carpenter was more than a trade, it was a calling. He was using his skills, his experience, and his emotions to craft something that would reflect his devotion to God and would enable people for years to come to acknowledge the presence of a loving God. His colleague, Avram, a very proficient goldsmith, would probably get the credit for the job in the long run, while his handiwork would be hidden, but he would always know that he had done his best and this table would be an offering of devotion.

Eldad had to work closely with Avram and his team of goldsmiths, because some gold rings were to be fitted to the timber on each of the four corners. Portability was important for the finished product so Eldad needed to construct some solid acacia wood poles that would be overlaid with gold, then fitted through the rings, making it possible for the table to be lifted and carried. In the meantime, the goldsmiths were also working on fashioning plates, dishes, bowls and pitchers, that were to be placed on the table and used, when it was completed, to bring drink offerings to God.

The craggy peaks of Mt Sinai towered over the camp where Eldad and the others were working. They had been there for a while waiting for instructions on the next stage of their journey. So it was a surprise when Moses called everyone together, and rather than giving travelling instructions, had initiated a building program. Moses had called on skilled workers to contribute to the project, but had also invited the people to make freewill donations of gold, silver and bronze, jewelery, fine linen, and anything else that would assist in achieving the finished product.

Eldad quickly volunteered his expertise as a carpenter but the whole family had gotten together to discuss what they could offer. Even the children excitedly entered into the conversation, discussing what they could contribute. They all agreed that if the one who had saved them from slavery and was leading them to a new hope and a new future wanted their father and husband to make a table to show that he was present with them, surely, they should give all they could in return. As a result, every evening they excitedly gathered around Eldad to ask how the building was going.

When his work was done, Eldad stopped and looked around at the hive of industry that was going on all around him. Not only were the goldsmiths at work, but other carpenters were also shaping acacia wood into frames that would hold the structure together, leather workers and needle-workers seemed to be busy with various types of material, and bronze-workers were also hard at work in another area of the camp. Everywhere he looked a mass volunteer workforce was focused on a single purpose, to create a place where their Maker would be made to feel at home.

That night the children ran out to meet Eldad as he returned to his tent. He kissed his wife and they sat down together and listened to him telling about the day's work. They heard the pride in his voice, and saw the smile on his face as he talked about the sense of satisfaction he had in using his skills to build the table. But they also noticed something else. He was excited at the way in which his table was part of a bigger picture; that he was part of a team of

A Place to Host the Maker

people who were working together to achieve a unified purpose that would assure anyone who came near their camp, that God was present at all times. Somehow Eldad sensed that his own creativity reflected the one who was the maker of heaven and earth, and that he had the privilege of creating a place that would host the maker.

You can read about this story for yourself at Exodus chapters 25 to 31.

A Pristine Destination

Perth, the capital city of Western Australia, is described as the world's most isolated continental capital city. Perth's nearest neighbor across the Indian Ocean to the west is Durban in South Africa, nearly 8000km away by plane. Jakarta, the capital of Indonesia is just over 3000km to the north, closer than Australia's own capital city of Canberra which is about 4000km to the east and a few hundred kilometers closer than Sydney, Australia's largest city. But if that seems isolated take a drive 1000km north of Perth to the tiny town of Carnarvon, home to about 5000 people, center of a thriving horticulture industry, and administrative base for the Gascoyne Region.

My wife Robyn and our two sons, Gavin and Dion, moved to Carnarvon in 1993 at the invitation of the Carnarvon Baptist Church in order that I could take up a role as a bi-vocational pastor. The church couldn't afford a full-time pastor, so part of the expectation in taking up the position was to find alternative employment. I brought into that community my experience as a journalist, and after some time as the founding editor of a weekly newspaper was engaged as marketing consultant to the Gascoyne Tourism Association. The membership of the association included hotel and accommodation providers, coach and airline companies, fishing and cruise operators, tour guides, cattle stations that were venturing into tourism, and a variety of small businesses that benefited from the tourist industry.

A Pristine Destination

While each of the members had a private goal of improving their own individual businesses and benefitting in some way from the tourist industry, all of them were aware that their success was dependent on the amazing natural beauty of the region in which they lived. As a group they recognized the role of the Association was to promote the region as a whole to the travelling and holidaying public and for that reason they had agreed as a group to engage a marketing consultant. Nevertheless, their personal goals were very high on their agenda.

Working jointly as a pastor and a marketing consultant made it a natural step to share the learnings across each discipline. The community of followers of Jesus, that we call the church, is a disparate group of people who are united by their faith, but like members of a tourist association, also had their own personal goals. And like the tourist association, my role as a pastor was to help people to get beyond simply establishing a great organization and to help people enter into a much deeper purpose that focused around something unique and beautiful.

The Gascoyne region takes in about 600km of Indian Ocean coastline which includes the Shark Bay World Heritage Area, the fishing port of Exmouth and the beautiful Ningaloo Reef, and inland to Mt Augustus, described in the quiz game Trivial Pursuit as the largest rock in the world. Ningaloo Reef is the world's largest fringing coral reef and each year is visited by the largest fish in the ocean, the gentle Whale Shark. The colorful coral reef stretches along the West Australian coast and is home to about 500 species of fish, graceful manta rays and turtles.

As the first marketing consultant to the Gascoyne Tourism Association, I had the job of telling the world about this amazing region of natural beauty and grandeur, but I also had the job of working with a disparate group of business people with competing interests and selfish motivations, to convince them to work together, pool their finances, expertise and knowledge, and find a way to build an industry in one of the most isolated parts of the planet. The added challenge was to do this in a sustainable way so that the region's natural beauty could be seen and experienced by humans without it being damaged in any way. This association of tourist operators, restaurateurs, small business operators and tourist-friendly pastoralists, needed to accept the role of host to tourists who would travel from many parts of the globe to experience an amazing destination.

The destination God's people need to share with our world is the invitation to dine with the consummate host. It's a pristine, beautiful message that is incomparable. The eternal God who created the world and all human beings, loved us with such a passion that he gave his only Son, Jesus, to make the supreme sacrifice of his own life. His love was so immense that God saw fit to choose sinful, selfish, and embarrassingly rebellious people, to make up a movement that was to change the world and usher in God's Kingdom.

But if the destination is so good, and I'm convinced there is no better destination, then why aren't churches full and overflowing? The main reason is that the church has not fully accepted its role as host. I see two issues that are illustrated from my tourism experience: Firstly, the creation of an institution that is often more interested in looking after itself than reaching out; and secondly, the people who make up this movement haven't worked out how to get people past that organization to see the destination.

For too long the church has been trying to get people to fit the organization; we've come at the situation with our institutions and their rules and in doing so, we've created artificial boundaries that have stopped people from seeing the destination. Our goal has been to get people into church and the expectations that we build around church are such that the destination is still out of view. The focus of the church has been inward, rather than outward.

The second problem we had with promoting our region was distance. The cost of airline travel was such that many other popular tourist destinations around Australia and even overseas, were able to compete for the traveler's dollar much more successfully. There was nothing wrong with the product we were selling, but the means of achieving that product was out of the reach of most people.

A Pristine Destination

A whole lot of people haven't had the opportunity to experience this beautiful, incomparable, amazing message of Jesus, because of distance. Many people are far from God and they either don't know he exists or the idea of being in a relationship with God the maker, the consummate host, hasn't even hit their radar.

When Paul wrote to the church in Ephesus, the words he used to describe their previous state included 'strangers', 'excluded' and 'foreigners'. He said they were far from God and were brought near by the blood of Christ. The community of God's people has a unique role of helping those who have previously felt excluded to feel welcome around the table of the Maker. As host, it is to be a welcoming community that draws others into the circle.

There is a third reason why people aren't drawn to eat at the Maker's table, and it's the same dilemma that was faced by the first people, Adam and Eve: The question of choice. As a tourism consultant, I was always aware that there were many people who would always prefer to travel to New York, Paris, or London, rather than come to our neck of the woods. Similarly, there will always be those who hear the good news of Jesus but choose not to accept the message. Even Jesus himself referred to the reality that few would accept his invitation, while many more would turn away.

After decades of travelling from slavery in Egypt to a land of hope, you would expect there would be a wholesale acceptance of the good life, but it wasn't the case. When the crunch came, fear, distrust and petty thinking ruled the day. Out of a group of twelve leaders who were appointed to spy out the Promised Land, only two saw the potential for the future, while the rest only saw giants.

Invitation to a New Land

How God the Maker, the consummate host, noticed that some people accepted his invitation to dine with enthusiasm but others thought the risk was too great.

A HUGE BUNCH OF grapes lay on the grass in front of them as Joshua and Caleb lay back and gorged themselves with fresh fruit. "I can't believe how good this is," Caleb mumbled through a mouthful of juicy grapes.

"And did you see those figs?" Joshua added. "I've never seen fruit like this. All that stuff we've been hearing about a land flowing with milk and honey was spot on."

"The big dudes were a bit scary, but the benefits outweigh the risks by a long shot," Caleb reflected as he weighed another bunch of grapes in his hand, eyeing off the purple orbs that filled his hand and cascaded over his fingers.

Joshua and Caleb had been sent across the Jordan River as spies to determine the best way to bring the Hebrew people into territory that had become known as "The Promised Land." The promise had gone back a long way. It started off with Abraham about 700 years earlier being told by God to leave his country in Mesopotamia and "go to the land of the Canaanites, Hittites, Amorites, Hivites and Jebusites—the land he swore to your ancestors to give you, a land flowing with milk and honey."

Invitation to a New Land

The promise had been renewed to Abraham's son Isaac, then to his grandson Jacob. Through various circumstances over time Abraham's descendants had found themselves in Egypt as slaves and through the leadership of Moses had escaped Egypt and made their way back to the Promised Land.

Although their fellow spies were more worried about the risks associated with this latest move, Joshua and Caleb were convinced their leader, Moses, was right in encouraging them to consider taking the people across the river to take possession of this new territory. From a military point of view there were certainly risks, but from an economic point of view the opportunities seemed limitless. What really convinced Joshua and Caleb, however, was the way in which stories about this promise had been repeated throughout their childhood, and were now part of the bed-time routine they had developed with their own children. It seemed the promise was coming to fulfilment at last.

As Joshua and Caleb enjoyed the fruit of the country they had been sent into as spies, they reflected on all that had happened leading up to this event. Like a consummate host, God had been planning this event for hundreds of years and had been inviting his people to come and eat with him. At last the planning and preparation was over and the dinner party was about to begin. Little did they know it would be another forty years before they would finally be able to bring the people across the river to take possession of the land.

One of the highlights of their journey from Egypt had been God's presence with them. He had instructed Moses to build a tabernacle, a kind of mobile worship center made primarily out of animal skins. When the people set up camp, the tabernacle was at the center of the camp, and when they moved it would be packed up and transported with them to the next camping place. The tabernacle represented God's presence with them as they travelled. It seemed to Joshua and Caleb that the God who had made the initial promise to Abraham was not a leader who simply made rules and orders then hid in some heavenly site office. He had plans, he motivated and resourced people to carry out those plans, and he travelled with them as they brought those plans into fruition. This was the kind of leadership they wanted to copy as they discussed the next stage of their journey, and it was the kind of leadership they wanted to model to the next generation.

This kind of leadership that was epitomized by a leader who lived with them in their journeys had become evident in a number of ways during their journey from Egypt. Joshua and Caleb discussed the way in which God had led them out of Egypt using a cloud in the day and a pillar of fire at night. This "presence" went ahead of them until the Egyptian soldiers began to follow them as they approached the Red Sea, and at that time, the cloud moved behind them creating a massive shadow that delayed the Egyptians in their nighttime assault. Their host didn't just lead from the front, but knew when leadership from behind was the safest option for those he was leading.

Their host's invitation to "come and eat with me" marked the other highlight of their journey. As Joshua and Caleb marveled at this "land of milk and honey" in which they found themselves, they reminisced about their experiences of recent times. There was plenty of food in Egypt. The Nile River produced an amazing array of fish, but the land also produced food as varied as cucumbers, melons, leeks, onions and garlic. But as they travelled through the desert they would have gone hungry if God hadn't provided food. In fact, it got so bad that people began complaining as they remembered all the food they had available to them in Egypt.

They talked about the time God had provided quails and manna when they didn't know where they were going to get their next meal. Throughout their travels the food provided by God had sustained them and now the spies were in the "land flowing with milk and honey" and were overwhelmed at the sort of food that was available for them. The consummate host had thought of everything.

"Everything's perfect." Joshua sighed, leaning back on a sturdy tree. "What could go wrong?"

"Well there's the other spies," Caleb responded. "I heard them talking. They're not convinced by milk and honey . . . not even the grapes and figs for that matter. They reckon the armies will be too hard to defeat."

Joshua rubbed his hand through his hair: "So claiming the promised land isn't just a simple case of claiming the promised land?"

"No," Caleb replied. "God's been promising this for ages, and here it is, but I think we're going to have to do some hard talking to convince the other guys."

The two spies got up from their comfortable hideaway in the river bed and began walking back to where the other spies were gathered. They were satisfied with their decision to claim the land, but they were preparing themselves for opposition from their colleagues. They had a sense that their God, the consummate host, had prepared the way for generations but the opportunity for claiming his promises may be stymied by people whose faith was darkened by fear and doubt.

You can read the story for yourself at Numbers chapter 13.

The Richest of Fare

I SAID IN THE introduction of this book that my wife and I, in recent years, have become keen cruise ship travelers. Talk to anyone who goes on cruises and it won't be long before the topic of food is raised. Normally, one pays their charges well before the trip, so during the cruise you can drop into the buffet at almost any time of the day or night and there is food of all kinds calling out to the passengers, 'eat me, eat me', and there is a temptation to think you're eating "for free."

This seems to me to be slightly different to the experience you have when you go to a restaurant and there on the menu you will notice a price alongside each individual dish. But what is it that causes this difference? I would suggest it is to do with a transaction. At the restaurant, there is a transaction since you decide about what you are going to eat on the basis of how much it will cost. The cruise ship buffet, on the other hand, seems to be only about consuming without limit.

We've come to an important stage in this book in terms of the stories we have been telling from the Bible. Up to now, all the stories have come from the Old Testament, a series of books that include theology, history, poetry and prophecy. From now on, our focus is on the New Testament which is a shorter set of books that focus on the time of Jesus and thereafter.

There was a period of about 400 years between the writing of the Old Testament and the writings of the New Testament. While the New Testament begins by providing detailed information about Jesus and includes information and writings after the time of Jesus, the Old Testament serves as an important lead-up to the time of Jesus. One of those who had a big influence in his writings was a man by the name of Isaiah who was a prophet and a prolific writer, who lived in the 8th century BCE. Later writers, as well as Jesus, drew on his writings as preparatory material for the coming of Jesus.

A number of Isaiah's prophecies have been called "servant songs" as they speak about a suffering servant who is to come to bring justice on the earth. These songs are usually interpreted as referring to the coming of Jesus as the Messiah. Shortly after the last of these four songs, Isaiah continues by making a profound statement that represents God's invitation to his people, an invitation to join him at his banqueting table.

> "Come, all you who are thirsty, come to the waters; and you who have no money, come, buy and eat! Come, buy wine and milk without money and without cost. Why spend money on what is not bread, and your labor on what does not satisfy? Listen, listen to me, and eat what is good, and you will delight in the richest of fare. Give ear and come to me; listen, that you may live. I will make an everlasting covenant with you, my faithful love promised to David. Isaiah 55:1-2

While this is an invitation to sit around the Maker's table it is also an invitation to a transaction. We are invited to come, buy and eat, but as we take that step towards God, he takes a step towards us, arms outstretched, and makes an everlasting covenant with us - a covenant of faithful love.

When Adam and Eve had the opportunity to take a step towards God they chose instead to take a step backward. When their son Cain had the opportunity to take a step towards God, he took a step backwards. Down through history people have been given the opportunity to take a step towards God, to come, buy and eat. Those of us who have decided to take that step towards God, have discovered God taking a step towards us. In fact, He's been there all the time holding out his hand in invitation, but as He steps towards us in response to our step, he makes an astounding offer of an everlasting covenant of faithful love.

Prominent New Testament scholar and author NT Wright explains how Isaiah's writings provide a summary of the big story about God and his interactions with humanity:

> Isaiah 40–55 sets out on a grand scale the purpose of Israel's God, YHWH, to reveal his sovereign power, his lordship over the kingdoms of the world, his reality over against the hollowness of the idols of the world, to demonstrate in action that he is true to his word as the creator and as the covenant God. He will do this, more specifically, by rescuing his people Israel from their exile in Babylon and by making them, in addition, a light to the nations, with the eventual result of the renewal of all creation. [1]

Through Abraham, the Hebrew people were promised the opportunity to become a great nation and they were promised their own land. When they came to that land from Egypt, spies were sent in to determine what action they should take and some of the spies felt that the risks were too great and reported this back to the people. The result of their decision was that they were destined to wander in the desert for the next forty years and most of the people would never experience God's hospitality in this new promised land.

The promises of hospitality that were recorded in the Old Testament lead to one person, Jesus, and his very first miracle occurred within the context of hospitality. Jesus was not the host of the wedding dinner, but as a guest he stepped up at the request of his mother, to resolve a potential embarrassment for the host and his family if the wine had run out. Someone who was essentially a minor guest of the wedding had taken on one of the responsibilities of the host.

The rest of this book highlights stories of hospitality from the New Testament, particularly focusing on Jesus. As we continue through the New Testament and learn more about Jesus we

---

1. Wright, N.T. *The Ear of the Servant*.

discover that hospitality is still at the heart of this grand story. One of the memorable stories of hospitality centers around the last supper that Jesus had with his disciples prior to him being betrayed by one of his closest friends, Judas. The Passover meal was prepared in advance and Jesus spent some intimate hours with his friends celebrating their favorite Jewish feast and preparing mentally for the events of the next few days.

After Jesus' death and resurrection, he met with two of his disciples and revealed himself to them during a meal. On another occasion he called his disciples together for a simple breakfast of fish and bread on the beach and used this time to challenge Peter about his priorities. That was certainly an opportunity for them to think back on the years they had spent with him and to realize that breakfast on the beach was typical of the way Jesus used hospitality to bring enlightenment.

Throughout those years Jesus told them stories about banquets as a way of explaining the Kingdom that he had come to introduce. He gave practical examples of what that Kingdom would look like, as he participated in meals and celebrations with people from a wide socio-economic spectrum. He even fed large crowds of people, and in that process taught his disciples, and anyone else who cared to notice, that he had an eternal purpose.

Through the life and death of Jesus, God invites us to eat at his table. It's not a free meal where we can gorge ourselves on his goodness, but it is a transaction. We are invited to join him at his table, but as we do so we recognize there are some responsibilities we need to accept, and that step towards him is not always without pain. In a fresh way Jesus shows what it means to join him at his table.

Come and Taste the Wine

How God the Maker, the consummate host stepped down from the role of host and became a guest, creating change from within.

MARY WAS EXCITED. SHE had been looking forward to this wedding for a long time. Now at last the time had come, and she watched with pride as the bride and bridegroom danced and celebrated with the other guests.

She had known the bride all her life and she couldn't take her eyes off her as she and her friends recounted stories to each other of this girl who had grown up in their village so close to all of them. They remembered when her mother had given birth and told stories of their own experiences of childbirth the same year. Now their sons and daughters were a part of the celebration and the women chatted together proudly as they surveyed the scene noting the way their children all got on so well.

Mary's boy, Jesus, was there with a group of his friends gathered around him, hanging on every word he spoke. He had grown into a handsome young man, and she looked around the room wondering which of the young women may one day become his wife. Yet somehow there seemed to be something about him that caused Mary to wonder what the future may hold. From the time of his birth she knew that Jesus had been set apart by God for something unique. She had watched him grow up, help Joseph as they fashioned furniture out of wood, then slip away whenever he had the chance to sit at the feet of the rabbis in the synagogue. None of his friends were like him in the way he dedicated himself to learning the Scriptures.

While the guests enjoyed themselves, the little group of matchmakers maintained their place in the corner of the room where they could keep a watchful eye on their sons and daughters. For a moment they stopped talking as there seemed to be a commotion coming from the other side of the room. The host was moving about the room and seemed to be quite distressed.

"What's the matter, Jonas?" Mary called as the host strode past them on his way to the kitchen.

"The wine's running out," he retorted. "I'm sure I ordered enough, but after two days I guess it's not surprising. I've got to do something quickly or the feast will be over, and I will be the laughing stock of all my friends."

Once again the women's heads came together as they discussed the predicament. It was unheard of for the wine to run out so early in the feast. As they talked, Mary withdrew quietly from the group. For a moment she stepped outside into the fresh air as she thought about a possible course of action. She knew that somehow Jesus would have a solution to the problem, but she didn't want him to think she was a busybody. She went back into the room and made her way through the guests to where Jesus was laughing and talking with a group of friends. She tugged at his sleeve and beckoned him to a quiet corner of the room.

"The wine has run out," she told Jesus. "You've got to do something. You can do something can't you?"

Jesus looked at her and sighed. He was enjoying the banquet and while he knew there would come a time when he would need to begin the ministry, this didn't seem to be the right time.

"It's not my time yet, mother," he said. "I'm sure Jonas has things under control."

"No, he hasn't," Mary replied. You need to do something or the whole banquet will be a disaster. These are your friends, your family. You grew up with them. You can't let them down now."

Mary could hear Jonas' voice getting louder in the back room as he tried to resolve the problem. As he rushed by her, Mary grabbed his coat and stopped him in his tracks.

"Jonas, it's all right. Calm down. Jesus will help you."

He paused and looked at Mary, then looked at Jesus. He had known Jesus since he was a boy. How could this young man solve a problem that he, an elder, couldn't solve? But he had always respected Jesus as he grew up. He was different from the other boys and he had a feeling that Mary might know what she was talking about.

"I'm the host here; Jesus is a guest," Jonas muttered as he rushed off.

Mary called over two of the young men who were assisting at the banquet. Jonas had been ordering them to find a solution to the problem and they looked distressed: "Do whatever Jesus tells you," Mary told them.

The young men looked furtively in the direction of Jonas. They wouldn't normally take instructions from someone other than the host, but Mary spoke quite authoritatively and they were desperate. They looked towards the young man who stood near Mary, wondering what he would suggest.

"Fill up these jars with water," Jesus told them.

The young men quickly began filling up the six large stone jars that stood in the corner of the room. It made no sense to them to be filling the jars with water when the real problem was a shortage of wine. When they had finished they came back to Jesus and asked him if there was anything else.

"Now dip a cup into the jars and take it to Jonas," Jesus instructed.

"Now we're playing silly games," the young men mumbled to each other, but did what they were told. As they took the cup out of the jar they could see the colour of the liquid they had drawn out of the jars. They sniffed at the cup. This was wine, and they could tell it was good wine. They were astounded because they had put the water into the jars. No-one else except Jesus and Mary and some of Jesus' friends had seen what they were doing. It wasn't a mistake.

One of the young men went up to Jonas with the cup of wine and gave it to him: "Sir, we have been able to get some more wine. I hope this meets your expectations."

Jonas held the cup under his nose and smelt the aroma before he took a sip. His eyes widened and he swirled the wine around in his mouth, then licked his lips.

"This is amazing wine," he said. "Most people give the best wine at the beginning then bring in the cheaper wine at the end of the banquet when everyone's too drunk to notice the difference. But this is the most beautiful wine I have tasted. Quickly, go and fill people's glasses. This banquet is really about to begin."

The young men rushed off and began filling people's empty glasses from the stone water jars. Every time they dipped into the jar they were amazed at the result. They smiled at each other as they heard the gasps from the wedding guests when they took their first sip of the new wine. This was their secret, but they knew that something amazing had just occurred, and Jesus had somehow been responsible for what could only be described as a miracle.

As Mary joined the other women still chattering in the corner of the room, she smiled to herself. Her friends hadn't noticed what had been going on so she joined in the conversation virtually unnoticed. She glanced across at her son, and their eyes met momentarily. Something significant was about to happen in the life of this special young man.

You can read this story for yourself at John chapter 2

Who is This Man?

THE ANCIENT CITY OF Chalcedon, now a district of Istanbul in Turkey, was the center of a major conference back in the year 451AD. Church leaders from a range of traditions travelled to Chalcedon from all over Europe and Asia to have a meeting about the nature of Christ. There was a lot of concern about the teaching of a man named Eutyches who was responsible for more than 300 monks just out of Constantinople, and who appeared to confuse the divine and human nature of God. A council was established to address what was considered a heresy, and come to some agreement about the question. The outcome of the Council of Chalcedon was the development of the Chalcedonian Creed which affirmed that Christ was fully human and fully divine, "the same perfect in Godhead and also perfect in manhood."

The reason I'm talking about this conference some 1500 years ago, is to highlight the fact that the question of the identity of Jesus has attracted controversy for a long time, but there has also been general acceptance that Jesus was not just a great prophet or wise leader, but is God in the flesh. All of the characteristics of God that we have already discovered as we have worked our way through the Old Testament are evident in Jesus as we now come to reflect on stories of hospitality in the New Testament. As we have observed God's role as host in calling us to his table, we will observe the same characteristics in Jesus.

The interchange between host and guest that was evident in the Old Testament is also evident in the New Testament as we

Who is This Man?

look at the life of Jesus. Theologian and ethicist, Dr Christine Pohl speaks of this as she highlights the example that Jesus sets for his followers.

> Jesus, who was dependent on the hospitality of others during much of his earthly sojourn, also served as the gracious host in his words and in his actions. Those who turned to him found welcome and rest and the promise of reception into the Kingdom. Jesus urged his human hosts to open their banquets and dinner tables to more than family and friends who could return the favor, to give generous welcome come to the poor and sick who had little to offer in return. Jesus promised that welcoming the stranger, feeding the hungry person, and visiting the sick were acts of personal kindness to the Son of man himself.[1]

Pohl says we make a habit of hospitality when we remember how much Jesus is present in the practice. She says our responses are shaped by the knowledge that Christ comes to us in the "stranger's guise." While we see Christ in strangers and guests, hospitality also allows us to act as Jesus to those guests.

One of the significant things about Jesus was the way in which he addressed matters from a point of view that was very different to what was generally accepted. Again and again he quietly, but firmly, turned the tables on commonly held ideals. Author of a number of significant books on the historical Jesus, Dr Ben Meyer explains that in Jesus' day a person wouldn't eat with someone of a different social standing, nor with someone of a different religion, but Jesus took a different view.

> The act of Jesus was to reverse this structure: communion first, conversion second. His table fellowship with sinners implied no acquiescence in their sins, for the gratuity of the reign of God cancelled none of its demands. But in a world in which sinners stood ineluctably condemned, Jesus' openness to them was irresistible. Contact triggered repentance; conversion flowered from communion. In

---

1. Pohl. *Making Room.* 92–93

the tense little world of ancient Palestine, where religious meanings were the warp and woof of the social order, this was a potent phenomenon.[2]

It was his special nature of being fully God and yet fully man, that enabled Jesus to stand apart from the culture of his day while still living within the confines of that culture. Yet, while this was the case there was nothing about his actions that weren't capable of being fully reproduced by his followers, both then, and into the future.

Jesus' interaction with a tax collector by the name of Zacchaeus was typical of the way in which he could draw close to people in the most natural and simple way, often through a meal or an act of hospitality, leading to a response that was quite extraordinary. We often hold to the view that if we see the need for someone to change because their behavior doesn't fit with our ideals, we need to speak to them directly about our concerns. The problem is our attempt to correct a person's behavior is usually seen as judgment no matter how much we may try to tell them we are speaking to them in love.

In Jesus' act of mercy he did not condemn or judge a man who was widely known for his shady financial dealings but sought his hospitality. It is interesting that it wasn't the other way around. Jesus didn't invite Zacchaeus to have coffee with him or to meet at a place where he could show that he was the one in control of the situation, rather he gave Zacchaeus the opportunity to host Jesus at his own home. It was through this curious act of hospitality, that Zacchaeus recognized his problem and came up with his own solution.

Zacchaeus' sin was related to the way he handled money, and his solution addressed the matter directly. He came up with two ways of proving that his lifestyle was to change for good as a result of his interaction with Jesus. Firstly, he would give half his possessions to the poor, an act that went against everything for which he was known. Secondly, he agreed to pay back four times

---

2. Meyer. The Aims of Jesus. 61

the amount to anybody he had cheated. Together, these solutions were likely to send Zacchaeus bankrupt, but such was the extent to which his hospitality of Jesus had impacted his life.

As Maker invites us to eat with him, like Zacchaeus, we recognize the need to invite Jesus into our home. This is a place where our privacy is laid bare before one who is fully God and fully man. A time when we open ourselves up to his gaze and the places we hold most dear are seen with clarity, yet without judgement. And as we sit in his presence, something happens that necessitates a response. Perhaps that is why so many people refuse the invitation, because they know the response they need to make is too hard to make. Yet in his presence there is a compulsion that leads us to realize we can no longer remain the same.

An Invitation Up a Tree

How God the Maker, the consummate host, allowed himself to become the guest of someone who didn't deserve his presence.

THERE WAS WORD ON the streets that Jesus would be in town shortly. The town gossips were working overtime as they relayed stories they had heard about this young man who seemed to be causing so much excitement. Everywhere he went crowds followed and there were stories about healings, demons being cast out and other miraculous events. Each story seemed to get more and more bizarre in the telling, and no one was really sure who to believe.

From his position in the market place Zacchaeus got to hear all the stories, but he knew which of the passers-by were known for embellishing their stories, and he could generally work out how much truth lay in the stories he overheard each day. From all that he had picked up it seemed that it could be worthwhile investigating this stranger a little more closely.

Zacchaeus was a tax collector. He was employed by the Roman government but his job required him to levy taxes against his fellow Jews. Naturally this attracted a fair bit of criticism, but it wasn't just the taxing that made him so unpopular. It was fairly normal procedure for tax collectors to carry out some creative accounting to benefit themselves, and Zacchaeus was one of the best.

An Invitation Up a Tree

He had accumulated a great deal of wealth and was well known as one of the fat cats of Jericho.

There seemed to be an unusual level of excitement in the marketplace this day. Little groups of people were gathering to talk while anxiously looking down the street. He could see a crowd gathering in the direction they were looking and noticed people heading in the direction of the disturbance. He called out to someone running past:

"Hey, where are you going? What's happening?"

"Apparently Jesus is down here. No point you seeing him. He wouldn't want anything to do with your type."

Zacchaeus' interest in Jesus had been sparked when he first heard the stories in the marketplace and there was something about them that made him want to know more. It wasn't like him to take an interest in anything other than his finances and how to further himself in the business world, but something was niggling at him.

Finally, he found himself getting up from his seat and heading down the street towards the crowd of people that had now gathered near a huge ficus tree.

He couldn't see Jesus, and being fairly short, struggled to get a view past the people who were pushing and shoving each other, anxious to get their own place near the front of the crowd.

Zacchaeus was a canny businessman, and he knew a thing or two about how to get around obstacles. He skirted the noisy crowd and jumped, reaching for the lowest branch of the tree. With a couple of deft moves, he found an ideal spot in the low branches where he could see exactly what was going on, and with a bit of luck, was out of sight of any of his many detractors.

He could barely hear what Jesus was saying with the noise of the crowd below him, but he noticed that Jesus was slowly walking along the road and was getting closer to the tree, so he hoped that he would begin to catch his words.

Then something happened. Jesus was now within earshot and as Zacchaeus reached forward to hear his words a little better, Jesus looked up.

Oh no. He had been seen. Not only was Jesus looking up, but the people around him followed Jesus' gaze and looked up as well.

To his astonishment, Zacchaeus realized that Jesus was speaking directly to him. "Zacchaeus, come down immediately. I must stay at your house today."

He didn't know what to think or how to react, but in a flash, Zacchaeus was down from the tree and started to escort Jesus back to his house.

He could hear the muttering in the crowd, but it didn't worry Zacchaeus. He was used to it. He recognized a couple of people in the crowd as men he had dealings with in the past. They were quite close and obviously raised their voices so that both Jesus and Zacchaeus could hear them grumbling: "He has gone to be the guest of a sinner."

Zacchaeus had no time to think about whether there was any food in the house, or what he would offer Jesus, but there was something so compelling in Jesus' voice, and he knew this man had something that he needed more than anything.

He desperately wanted to host Jesus in his home, but at the same time there was an overwhelming feeling of guilt because never in his life had he done something for another without an expectation of what he would get in return.

There was something about Jesus that stirred him deep within, bringing to the surface a feeling that was completely new. For the first time in his life Zacchaeus was responding to an invitation to give of himself to another; to be the host instead of being the recipient of service.

They came to the front door of his house, and barely thinking about what he was about to say, Zacchaeus stopped in his tracks, looked Jesus in the eye and uttered some words that were totally out of character. He wasn't even sure where the words came from, but Jesus' request—no, maybe it wasn't even a request—had stirred his heart and mind in a way he never before experienced.

"Look, Lord! Here and now I give half of my possessions to the poor, and if I have cheated anybody out of anything, I will pay back four times the amount."

An Invitation Up a Tree

The statement was not only out of character, but to the people who gathered around it was almost preposterous. "If I have cheated anybody out of anything." This was a confession. An admission of guilt. Before the words came out of his mouth the lawyers were rubbing their hands together.

And as for giving money to the poor. Zacchaeus was the last person to give any consideration to anyone less fortunate than himself.

The crowd fell silent as they waited to see how Jesus would respond. Mothers reached down to quieten their children; people anxiously tried to lean forward so they wouldn't miss what would come next.

Jesus looked Zacchaeus in the eye, then turned to the crowd and announced: "Today salvation has come to this house, because this man, too, is a son of Abraham. For the Son of Man came to seek and to save the lost."

You can read this story for yourself at Luke chapter 19

A Third Culture

As a young theological student, I don't think I had much of a clue about what to expect from theological studies. There were so many new things to learn, not to mention the whole experience of studying at a tertiary level. Every so often significant theologians or speakers would visit our city and students were encouraged to attend then report back to our lecturers on what we had learned. I had no idea what Liberation Theology was when we told of the visit of René Padilla, but I duly accepted the recommendation of the seminary and went to hear what it was all about.

René Padilla, it turned out, was a leading South American theologian and missiologist who advocated Liberation Theology from an evangelical perspective and was promoting the dual priorities of evangelism and social activism. This was fairly controversial in evangelical circles at the time, and I discovered that some of my fellow students found his approach too radical. Having come from a background where I had a strong association with indigenous communities, I was entranced by his message and began to research the issues of social justice at a deeper level.

More than three decades later I came across the writings of Padilla's daughter, Ruth Padilla DeBorst and was similarly fascinated by the fact her language about the invitation to God's table was not dissimilar from my own thinking. DeBorst, who with her husband James Padilla DeBorst leads the Comunidad de Studios Tologicos Interdisciplinarios in San Jose, Costa Rica, and has developed a reputation as an evangelical theologian in her own right, describes the followers of Jesus as third culture people.

In an article in the *Evangelical Review of Theology*, De Borst explains that while the follower of Jesus is embedded in her or his own national, ethnic and cultural stories, they belong to another reality, the second culture, in which they inhabit the story of God's action and mission in relation to the world. This creates what she calls a 'double–belonging' in which a new third culture is created. Allegiance to this third culture gives a person freedom to look at their own national, ethnic or cultural group from an external vantage point, and they no longer view their own cultural environment as an all-determining reality.

> As 'third-culture' people, Christians are called to celebrate their unmerited inclusion at God's kingdom table and stand in the often painful place of the prophet, denouncing national, class, ethnic and tribal values and practices that counter God's good purposes for all people, even at the risk of exclusion, ridicule, persecution or death.[1]

De Borst claims that once the follower of Jesus has captured a vision of the table of God's kingdom and submitted to Christ's sovereignty, and are filled with the Holy Spirit, they are able to both welcome people who look, think, speak and eat differently than they do, and also take the risk of confronting any power that excludes or deprives people of their rightful presence at the table. This capacity, she says, is because followers of Jesus are called to acknowledge they have been sent as he was into the world, as agents of reconciliation.

This is a radical approach to the Christian faith, but is in keeping with the teachings and example of Jesus who challenged people's thinking about a range of issues. In a meal he held with a group of religious and civic leaders, Jesus challenged the whole idea of social class, bringing to their attention the problems associated with judging others because of their status in society, or even

---

1. DeBorst. *Unexpected Guests*. 74

their health or wellbeing. He used the example of people who sit close to the host of a dinner party to try and prove their respected place in society. Jesus' teaching on humility went right against current trends.

During this meal Jesus told the guests a story about a man who put on a banquet, but nobody turned up because of other engagements. Instead of cancelling the meal, the host invited a whole lot of people who were sick, unpopular, and isolated and brought them in to enjoy the meal. This wouldn't have been received well by the group Jesus was talking to because they prided themselves on their place in society and who they considered to be acceptable for their group.

De Borst says about this story that it confronts the official storyline of the rich and powerful, and springs from and extends the long story of God's good purposes for all people that all Jews would have recognized as part of their tradition.

> In his prophetic role, Jesus is spearheading a mission of renewal among his people that builds on God's mission of reestablishing the relational, creational image of God in all people, which is being threatened by human sin, by imperial power, and by legalistic and ritualistic religious power.[2]

Australian theologian, Graham Hill in his book, *Global Church* adds to this when he says that many Majority World thinkers agree that hospitality is crucial for the mission of the church. He says that through hospitality and welcome the church positions itself as an alternative culture, a culture that reveals God's Kingdom.

> Such hospitality connects with the marginal, the broken, the rejected, the excluded and the despised. It fosters a spirituality of partnership, hospitality and inclusivity. It welcomes people into God's family. Hospitality demonstrates the extraordinary grace of Jesus Christ to the world.[3]

2. DeBorst. *Unexpected Guests.* 74
3. Hill. *GlobalChurch.* 1555–1556

A Third Culture

It is this grace that sets followers of Jesus apart from those who are simply trying to do good out of a sense of shared humanness. Grace makes it possible to love the unlovely, to show kindness to the greedy, and to forgive the unforgiveable. Grace makes it possible to turn cultural standards upside down as Jesus was able to do in his day.

As we humbly accept the invitation to sit at the table with our Maker, not seeking the best seat, we discover that it is not necessarily a comfortable place to sit. While we may be overwhelmed at the grace that has made it possible for us to sit at his table, and be filled with thanksgiving, there is a discomfort that is necessary as we realize the responsibilities that come with that seat. Suddenly, our view of the world is colored by that grace.

The Story of the Great Banquet

How God the Maker, the consummate host, explained some principles to be followed by both guests and hosts.

ELIAS WAS DELIGHTED THAT he had been invited to dinner with his friend Matthias. He had been talking about this dinner for a few weeks since Jesus had accepted Matthias' invitation to come and dine with him, and he had been busy since then inviting the other Pharisees in their group to join them.

At last, the time had come and they had all gathered at Matthias' house with a sense of expectation because Jesus had become a popular figure locally, but there were a lot of questions about him. Matthias, Elias and the other were quite suspicious of Jesus, but they figured that if he came to a meal with them it would give them an opportunity to ask some questions and find out a little bit more about him. It would also be an opportunity to test him.

They had arranged for a local man to sit just near the door of Matthias' house. His legs and arms were abnormally swollen and it was very clear to anyone who came near that he was suffering from his condition. Elias and Matthias winked at each other as Jesus approached. They were keen to see how he would respond to the man, particularly as it was the Sabbath.

Suddenly, Jesus was there in front of them, looking straight at them as he asked, "Is it lawful to heal on the Sabbath, or not?"

Elias was about to say something, then noticed Matthias looking at him, and give a small shake of the head. He swallowed. They wanted to test Jesus, but didn't want to enter into a conversation so soon. Jesus stood there for a minute waiting for a response from Elias, then moved towards the man. He knelt down next to him and quietly said something that Elias couldn't hear. As Jesus stood up and walked through the door into Matthias' house he looked at the wise men who had invited him to dinner and asked: "If your child, or even your ox, fell into a well on the Sabbath day, wouldn't you pull it out?"

Elias stood there unable to do anything. For the first time in his life someone who was less qualified than himself had come up with a question that he couldn't respond to immediately. Stunned by the question he was even more aghast as he saw the swelling on the man's legs start to subside. He watched the man for a while then turned to go into the house where already the other guests were jostling for the best seats.

Rubbing his hands through his beard, he turned and began walking towards his seat near Matthias. They always looked out for each other. Then unexpectedly, a hush fell over the group. It wasn't Matthias, the host of the dinner, calling them to order. It was Jesus, the guest, who was beginning to tell a story.

"When someone invites you to a wedding feast don't take the most honored place," Jesus was saying. All of a sudden Elias was feeling a little uneasy as he made his way to the seat next to Matthias. What was Jesus getting at here?

"You don't know that the host may have invited someone more distinguished and you'll be embarrassed if he has to ask you to move down the table to make way for someone else. Imagine what everyone would be saying," Jesus added. Those people who hadn't yet found a seat were nervously moving into the position, trying not to attract attention. They wondered what would come next.

"Here's an idea," Jesus said. Instead of taking the seat nearest the host, why not take the seat at the other end of the table, then when the host invites you to move up you will have been honored in front of all the guests instead of being embarrassed. Those who exalt themselves will be humbled and those who humble themselves will be exalted."

Elias was now feeling very uncomfortable as he took his seat next to Matthias. What Jesus was saying went against all his traditional views, but it seemed to make sense. But Jesus hadn't finished speaking. This time he was speaking directly to Matthias.

"When you put on a special meal don't just invite your relatives and your special friends," he said. Elias looked furtively around the room. He had been to many functions at Matthias' house and the guests were always the same. They were a tight bunch of friends and close relatives and they all had influence and money. Jesus was the only person in the room who was outside their usual group. Elias glanced at Matthias to see how he was coping with what Jesus was saying.

"When you give a banquet invite the cripple, the lame and the blind." Well, Matthias had invited the man with the swelling, Elias thought to himself, even if he was just a plant to test Jesus, and he certainly wouldn't have allowed him to come inside to eat. Jesus then made a rather cryptic comment, that Elias pondered for a moment: "These people won't be able to repay you, but you will be repaid at the resurrection of the righteous."

Elias tried to break the nervous tension in the room by announcing: "Blessed is the man who will eat at the feast in the Kingdom of God." Jesus responded to his statement immediately, and just like the great rabbis who Elias respected, Jesus was telling another story.

"A certain man was holding a great banquet and invited many guests," Jesus began. "When the time came for the banquet he sent out his servants to all the people who had been invited to remind them that the time for the banquet had arrived. But they all started to make excuses. One of them had bought a block of land and needed to go and inspect it, while another had bought some oxen and wanted to go and see if they could do the job for which he had bought them. Someone else said he had got married so wouldn't be able to attend the banquet."

The Story of the Great Banquet

Elias was listening to Jesus' story carefully, wondering where he was heading. As he looked around the room he could see that everyone was hanging on Jesus' words.

The story continued: "The servant went back to his master and reported on the replies he had received from those people who had been invited. The master was angry when he received the news from his servant, so he ordered the servant to go out into the streets and back lanes and invite the poor, the crippled, the blind and the lame and bring them to the banquet.

"Within a short time the servant returned and told his master that he had followed his orders, but people didn't seem to be willing to accept the invitation. 'Go to the country,' the master said. 'Find people on country roads and in the backwaters. I want my banquet to be full, and I'm telling you no-one who I originally invited will get to taste my banquet.'"

The room was silent as Jesus concluded his story. The guests shuffled nervously and Matthias quickly beckoned to the servants to start serving the guests to break the silence. Everything that Jesus had said had cut too close to the bone and Elias sensed that Matthias, sitting next to him, was feeling as uncomfortable as he was at that moment. Elias, Matthias and their friends had always aimed for the first, the best and the biggest. They had the best banquets and invited the most popular people. They aimed for the best places and were keen to be seen ahead of everyone else.

But this stranger, a guest at their banquet, had promoted humility, emphasized the significance of being last, and encouraged the acceptance of those people who were at the bottom of the popularity ladder. Everything that seemed important and normal was being challenged by this upstart. Elias turned to Matthias who brought his fist down on the table and called out to the assembled guests: "Come, my friends. Let's eat."

You can read this story for yourself at Luke chapter 14

Messy Hospitality

I FILLED MY PLATE and sat down at the table where I was able to quickly survey the scene in the church hall. I was at church on Saturday night and we were eating together; grandparents and grandchildren, toddlers and teenagers, older people who had been attending church for as long as they could remember, and young families with little or no church experience. There were people of various nationalities and all of them were excitedly connecting with each other as they filled their plates with food from a long row of tables at the end of the hall.

It was Messy Church, a congregation of our church that has been meeting once a month on a Saturday evening for about six years. Some of those who were there attend our traditional Sunday morning church service, some attend other churches, and for some it is their only experience of church. Each month we gather to do crafts or activities around a theme, we hear a Bible story and sing together, then enjoy a meal together.

Messy Church began in 2004 when a group of people at St Wilfrid's near Portsmouth United Kingdom, became frustrated that, as a church, they weren't effective in reaching children with God's story. One of the original team members, Lucy Moore, developed a model that has since grown into an international movement. In just over ten years 4000 Messy Churches were established in thirty-five countries and in twenty denominations. Messy Church has five key values, Christ-centered, all ages, celebration, creativity and hospitality.

In many ways the value of hospitality has been essential to the success of Messy Church as a fresh expression of church. Hospitality at Messy Church is described in this way: "It reflects a God of unconditional love and is a church for people outside church, providing an oasis of welcome and a safe space in which to thrive. Messy Church is about hospitality, expressed most evidently by eating together."

The book called the Acts of the Apostles in the New Testament describes the way the early church behaved. Pentecost is often described as the birth of the church and immediately after this event that is described in Acts chapter 2, we read that the people gathered together to do a range of things, including eating together.

> They devoted themselves to the apostles' teaching and to fellowship, to the breaking of bread and to prayer. Everyone was filled with awe at the many wonders and signs performed by the apostles. All the believers were together and had everything in common. They sold property and possessions to give to anyone who had need. Every day they continued to meet together in the temple courts. They broke bread in their homes and ate together with glad and sincere hearts, praising God and enjoying the favor of all the people. And the Lord added to their number daily those who were being saved (Acts 2:42–47).

From its very inception the church saw hospitality as central to its existence, along with teaching, fellowship, prayer and mutual support and fellowship. Is it any wonder that when the followers of Jesus come together today in a meaningful way, hospitality usually plays a key part? That has certainly been our experience in the way Messy Church has formed into a missional community in our location.

Various writers have acknowledged the value of hospitality as an act of grace within the Christian church. Australian missiologist and author, Michael Frost in *Surprise the World; The Five habits of Highly Missional People* describes eating as a central Christian practice since the beginning of the movement.

> And not only eating sacramentally, as in the Eucharist, but eating missionally as a way to express love to all. More than that, eating with others can be perceived as a profoundly theological practice. It mirrors the character of the Triune God.[1]

In their book *Right Here, Right Now*, authors Alan Hirsch and Lance Ford say that sharing meals together on a regular basis is one of the most sacred practices we can engage in as believers.

> Missional hospitality is a tremendous opportunity to extend the kingdom of God. We can literally eat our way into the kingdom of God! If every Christian household regularly invited a stranger or a poor person into their home for a meal once a week, we would literally change the world by eating![2]

Of course, there are many ways that this can occur, but some are more useful than others. Pot luck dinners and morning teas are an enjoyable aspect of church life, but they rarely fit into any intentional missional strategy. One of the great advantages of Messy Church is that hospitality is both intentional and deliberate. The shared meal is always a part of Messy Church and the way it is incorporated contributes to the theme and provides opportunity for disciple-making conversations.

Christine D Pohl says that hospitality won't occur in any significant way in our lives or churches unless we give it deliberate attention.

> Because the practice has been mostly forgotten and because it conflicts with a number of contemporary temporary values, we must intentionally nurture a commitment to hospitality. It must also be nurtured because the blessings and the benefits are not always immediately apparent. Hospitality becomes less difficult and more "natural"

---

1. Frost. *Surprise the World*. 122
2. Hirsch and Ford. *Right Here, Right Now*. 122

Messy Hospitality

as we grow more familiar with the practice. Grace and gift infuse it in ways that are not easily accounted for. We experience fulfillment as we give of ourselves, but we can neither explain nor anticipate it.[3]

While we need to be deliberate in the way we incorporate hospitality into our missional strategy, it also needs to be recognized that there are some risks. There is a significant cost in both finances and time in organizing the mission of the church around hospitality, but there is also the risk that people may not respond to this act of grace in the way we expect. Pohl explains that offering hospitality requires that we allow a place for uncertainty, contingency, and human tragedy. She says it is important to acknowledge the difficulty of hospitality.

> If Christians expect it to be easy to welcome strangers—that it will always involve competent hosts and grateful guests—they will be disappointed and will grow discouraged very quickly. Thinking that they have done something wrong or that they are not "good" at it, they will readily forsake the practice. One practitioner worries that people might abandon hospitality when it fails to produce the "expected" results within a given time frame. Hospitality will not occur in any significant way in our lives or churches unless we give it deliberate attention.[4]

When the need arose for Jesus to offer hospitality to a hungry crowd who had been following him, a seemingly accidental situation developed into a surprising deliberate act that can only be called a miracle. At a time of need, Jesus called on his disciples to address that need with whatever resources were available to them. As they stepped into the role of hosts, the disciples discovered that the grace of God was being administered to the crowd through their own hands. The unexpected occurred when the incompetent allowed the power of God to take control.

---

3. Pohl. *Making Room*. 92–93
4. Pohl. *Making Room*. 1927–1928

The Expanding Lunchbox

How God the Maker, the consummate host, intervened in a time of need, and in so doing showed his grace and creativity.

MICHAEL AND HIS FATHER were making their way down the hillside towards the village where they lived. It had been a long day but one of the most memorable days they had ever had. Father and son were quiet as they followed the stony path, their minds full of the events of the day. That morning mother had kissed them both goodbye, handed the lunchbox to Michael, and sent them on their way as they headed out to find the teacher they heard so much about.

    It had been a couple of days since father told Michael they were going to hear Jesus teaching. He couldn't wait and had told all his friends at school. They had heard about Jesus, too, and it was the main topic of conversation around the school yard. Some of the bigger boys said he was just a salesman and wasn't worth listening to, but others said their parents were quite in awe of him. Whatever anyone else said, Michael was keen to see Jesus for himself, and he knew that his father felt the same way.

    Finally, the day had come and Michael and his father headed off towards the lake. They had followed the instructions they had been given where to find Jesus, but it seemed that people had come from all the villages around to see him. There were people everywhere, but no one seemed to know where to go. Michael's father asked a few people if they had seen Jesus, then they heard a shout and noticed a boat coming in to shore. Sure enough it was Jesus and within a short time the boat pulled up on the beach and Jesus was calling on everyone to sit down so they could hear what he had to say.

As Michael picked up his pace to keep up with his father's long steps, he remembered how much the pair of them had enjoyed listening to Jesus. In fact, they were so engrossed they hadn't realized how quickly the time had gone. Before they knew it, they realized it was dinner time, and people around them were starting to get fidgety. It was a big crowd, Michael's father reckoned there were a few thousand people there. He was pretty good at working out that sort of thing, Michael thought to himself.

At one stage Michael remembered seeing Jesus having a discussion with his disciples, then the next thing some of the disciples were walking around the crowd asking if anyone had any food. He wasn't sure whether to mention the lunchbox mother had given him that morning, but he thought he should. He called out to Matthew who was nearby and said, "I've got five small loaves of bread and some sardines. Will that help?" Matthew gratefully took the lunchbox from him and took it back to Jesus.

"Why did you do that," his father said. "Now what are we going to have for dinner?"

"I don't know, but it seemed to be the right thing to do," Michael said. There was something quite compelling about Jesus, and to do something for him seemed to be the most natural thing to do at the time.

It didn't look like anybody else had any food to donate, because as he watched, Jesus took Michael's bread rolls and sardines, broke them into pieces and looked up to heaven and gave thanks to God for the food. The next thing, the disciples were walking amongst the crowd handing out pieces of bread and fish. What amazed Michael and his father as they watched was that each of the disciples seemed to have enough food to give to everyone. When one of them got to Michael and his father he handed them both some bread and fish, and it was enough to satisfy them. But he went on, and kept on handing out bread and fish to the people next to them. Nobody went hungry.

That was all pretty amazing, but after they had all eaten, the disciples went back around the crowd cleaning up the mess. Some people hadn't eaten all they had, and others had dropped some bread on the ground. Each of the disciples had a big basket and by the time they had finished, each of the baskets were full of the scraps. Michael couldn't believe what he was seeing. It had all come from his small lunchbox, yet there was more than enough food for everyone.

As they approached their village, Michael's father spoke. It was the first word he had spoken since they started their walk homewards, and Michael looked up at him, surprised.

"Something pretty amazing happened back then, don't you think, Michael?"

"Sure did, Father. You know how much food was in my lunchbox don't you? I mean that was a miracle that all that crowd was fed from the food in that box. I can't wait to get home and tell mother."

"Son, you have just seen the power of God at work. Don't ever forget that. We could have easily lasted without a meal and got something when we got home, but Jesus provided for us with the utmost generosity. It's like the old prayer says: 'give us this day our daily bread.'"

Michael hadn't heard his father talking like that before. He was a pretty down to earth sort of fellow and didn't often show his emotions. Somehow the events of the day had impacted his father in quite an unusual way.

"Come on, let's tell mother," Michael called as he broke into a run. "Last one home's a . . ."

Father didn't catch the last words, as Michael scampered off towards home. As he watched his son disappear into the front door he smiled to himself. They had shared an event that would remain with them both for the rest of their lives.

You can read this story for yourself at Luke chapter 9

The Birdwatcher and The Cross

THERE WERE ONLY TWO of us sitting in the lonely airport. He was a British bird watcher who was waiting for a change of planes before spending time in the remote Kimberley region of Western Australia where he hoped to spot some rare birds. I had a tip-off that he would have a short stop-over before catching a light plane to a pastoral station and was told where I would find him waiting for his flight. The airport waiting room was empty, but sure enough, I found an elderly gentleman sitting alone surrounded by a few items of baggage.

Many of the avid readers of the theological works of the late Dr John RW Stott would not be aware of his worldwide interest in bird-watching. Yet here I was far from any of the world's great theological halls, discussing birdwatching with a man who was named in Time magazine in 2005 one of the 100 most influential people in the world. Author of scores of books, and principle framer of the landmark Lausanne Covenant in 1974, John Stott developed a reputation as a leader of the evangelical movement worldwide.

Birds aside, John Stott's books on the cross of Christ are probably some of the most widely read and highly recognized of any written on the subject. In his book, *Basic Christianity*, Stott says: "The Bible isn't about people trying to discover God, but about God reaching out to find us." Perhaps, this is what I am implying in the idea that God has invited us to come and eat with him. Stott explains the expectation that comes with the invitation:

Come Eat With Me

"Jesus never concealed the fact that his religion included a demand as well as an offer. Indeed, the demand was as total as the offer was free. If he offered men his salvation, he also demanded their submission. He gave no encouragement whatever to thoughtless applicants for discipleship. He brought no pressure to bear on any inquirer. He sent irresponsible enthusiasts away empty.

"Luke tells of three men who either volunteered, or were invited, to follow Jesus; but no one passed the Lord's test. The rich young ruler, too, moral, earnest and attractive, who wanted eternal life on his own terms, went away sorrowful, with his riches intact but with neither life nor Christ as his possession . . . The Christian landscape is strewn with the wreckage of derelict, half-built towers—the ruins of those who began to build and were unable to finish. For thousands of people still ignore Christ's warning and undertake to follow him without first pausing to reflect on the cost of doing so.

"The result is the great scandal of Christendom today, so called 'nominal Christianity'. In countries to which Christian civilization has spread, large numbers of people have covered themselves with a decent, but thin, veneer of Christianity. They have allowed themselves to become somewhat involved, enough to be respectable but not enough to be uncomfortable. Their religion is a great, soft cushion. It protects them from the hard unpleasantness of life, while changing its place and shape to suit their convenience.

No wonder the cynics speak of hypocrites in the church and dismiss religion as escapism . . .The message of Jesus was very different. He never lowered his standards or modified his conditions to make his call more readily acceptable. He asked his first disciples, and he has asked every disciple since, to give him their thoughtful and total commitment. Nothing less than this will do.[1]

---

1. Stott. *Basic Christianity*.

The Birdwatcher and The Cross

If the Bible were a giant bicycle wheel, the cross is the hub around which everything else turns. Everything leads up to this event, and it points onward to the future. When God invites us to come eat with him, it is not simply to a banquet where we will feast, then walk away with full stomachs and a hearty laugh. He calls us to a deep relationship where we are able to share at the most intimate level, receiving the richest of fare from the Maker, and offering back to him our love and devotion.

The reality is that as we come to God we usually come, as Judas did, with a great deal of baggage. Just as Judas was hiding the knowledge that he had just betrayed the one he was sitting next to, so we may find ourselves at the table with the Maker and know deep down that we have betrayed him in more ways than we can count, and that really we have no right to accept his invitation. Yet graciously he reminds us of our betrayal and waits for us to respond to our conscience and the promptings of the Spirit of God.

Adam and Eve were given a choice of eating the fruit of hundreds, maybe thousands, of amazing fruit trees they were privileged to tend, and there was only one amongst them all that they were told to avoid. Yet they couldn't resist tasting the fruit from that one tree, contrary to God's warning. Their sons Cain and Abel had the opportunity to use their talents in animal husbandry and farming to honor God with their produce and provide for their families and friends. But Cain became jealous and one thing led to another before he killed his brother.

The cross of Christ stands at the center of history and it is through what Jesus did in his death and resurrection that made it possible for us to sit at the table with him, and receive his forgiveness and grace, and at the same time to make right decisions about how to behave in relation to God and the people who eat at the table with us. For that matter, it is the cross that also gives us the ability to work towards living in right relationship with those people who have chosen not to sit at the table with us. This is the radical nature of what it means to eat with our Maker.

The question is, what does the cross actually do? Evangelicals have generally used the word salvation to describe what happens to people as a result of the cross and their response to what Christ did at the cross. Salvation may be described in various ways but American philosopher Dallas Willard describes it as deliverance from sin.

> Salvation is, biblically speaking, deliverance. It is a condition of being delivered from sin and, with that, guilt—but primarily the emphasis is on being delivered from sin. How we understand that is what matters. Some people, of course, depending on their theory, understand it as in the penal theory: that now your sins are paid off and you have a kind of contract with God, you will not be punished for your sins. But in the biblical / New Testament picture, I think, what you have presented is salvation as a form of life [with God]. And that, I think, is what John and Paul and the New Testament generally understand it to be . . . that people now have a life from above, and their salvation, their deliverance, is a matter of having that life and living that life with God. Salvation is participating in a transforming friendship with the Trinity.[2]

This new life, this life of deliverance, is the privilege of being able to sit at the table with our Maker and partake of his banquet. Without the cross the invitation would have no influence; without the cross we would have neither the will nor the ability to accept the invitation. At the cross God signed off on his invitation, giving it the imprimatur of the consummate host.

One man who was about to discover that sitting at the table with the Maker was a joyless event without the power of the cross, was Judas, one of a group of twelve who were Jesus' closest friends in the three years leading up to the event of his crucifixion.

---

2. Willard. *Renewing the Christian Mind.* 198

Not Quite the Last Banquet

How God the Maker, the consummate host, graciously invited a traitor, amongst his other friends, to dine with him.

JUDAS WAS NERVOUS. JESUS had asked to celebrate the Passover with his friends, the group that had come to be known as The Twelve. Not that Judas didn't want to be involved but there were some things going on in the background that made him uncomfortable about spending too much time with Jesus. In recent days he had been doing his best to avoid him while not giving away too much.

A few of the Twelve had asked Jesus about what sort of preparation he wanted in order to celebrate the Passover. Why they weren't satisfied with celebrating the Passover in their own homes annoyed Judas a bit. It seemed that this was another time he would have to be with Jesus and the others and put on a good face. Right now he couldn't be seen to be undermining the happy little group of supporters so he went with them to Jesus to ask about preparations.

Surprisingly, Jesus seemed to be a step ahead of them. He told them to go into the city and explained the house they were to go to and the person they were to speak to about the Passover. He even gave them instructions about what to say: "My appointed time is near. I am going to celebrate the Passover with my disciples at your house."

Judas followed along with the other disciples. Peter and John, as usual were up front making themselves useful so he quietly followed along, trying not to make too much of his nonchalance.

When they got to the house, sure enough the man Jesus had told them about came to the door and to the surprise of the whole group, seemed to be expecting them. He showed them upstairs where they found preparations for the Passover were already underway. The smell of lamb and rosemary wafted into the room and the clattering of pots and pans indicated they weren't far from a busy kitchen. There wasn't that much to be done but the Twelve busied themselves in preparation for the meal, anxious to have everything in place by the time their host arrived.

It wasn't long before Jesus arrived and the Twelve found their place around the table. Judas thought he could find a spot at the end of the table where he wouldn't have to enter into too much conversation but somehow he found himself next to Jesus. This was embarrassing. Over the last few days Judas had been offered money to turn Jesus into the authorities and here he was sitting next to the very person he was about to betray. His mouth was dry and he tapped his foot on the ground and was about to try and make small talk when Jesus began to speak.

"Someone here is going to betray me," Jesus announced. Judas' heart missed a beat. He made sure his eyes didn't connect with any of the Twelve who were all looking at each other and asking the question, "surely it's not me?" Judas took advantage of the conversation so as not to look guilty by not responding like the other disciples, suddenly glad he was close to Jesus. He leaned over without making eye contact and joked, "You don't mean me do you Rabbi?" At the far end of the table two or three of the disciples were loudly discussing the dilemma and other members of the Twelve were nervously talking among themselves, so Judas took a deep breath when Jesus quietly leaned towards him and said, "You have said so."

Not Quite the Last Banquet

It was almost a relief to Judas that Jesus knew. His pulse was racing and his palms were sweaty but he knew that his time had come and he had to get out of the room as soon as possible. It seemed as if Jesus, the consummate host, had stage-managed this moment. Everything had been perfect up to that time, the preparation, the food, and even the timing. And to his relief it seemed the other disciples hadn't picked up on Jesus' words, "You have said so."

The fact that Jesus himself knew filled Judas with a crazy mixture of emotions. Regret, fear and anger surged through his veins as he thought about the thirty pieces of silver he had been given by the authorities, all the while desperately thinking how he could get out of the room without disturbing the solemnity of the moment.

Judas' memory of what happened yesterday still bristled with clarity. He had met with two senior figures of the religious bureaucracy in unusual circumstances. They had suggested a back street, well away from the busy heart of the city, and he had gone to the nominated spot in two minds. He felt trapped when he saw them approach him in the dark alley from two different directions, but he was shaking with excitement at the same time. A short conversation ensued and a small bag of coins changed hands.

Now that bag was burning a hole in Judas' pocket. He loved Jesus. They had travelled together, and a strong tie had developed. Jesus had even trusted Judas with the responsibility of looking after the money for the Twelve and it was in this area of trust that he was most vulnerable. He didn't know what would happen to Jesus in the next few hours but he had a foreboding that it wouldn't be good, and that he would have to bear the responsibility for whatever evil would occur.

The meal was nearly over and the rest of the Twelve were relishing this special time with their host, and enjoying each other's company as they remembered their people's history through each aspect of the Passover meal. Judas' stomach was churning. He

Come Eat With Me

glanced at Jesus and their eyes caught. Both love and disappointment showed as Jesus gazed back at the friend who had become a traitor. Judas knew it was time to leave.

You can read this story for yourself at Matthew chapter 26

The Meal that Unites

As a child I remember attending my grandmother's Baptist church where an interesting custom was maintained. At the end of the Sunday morning service a final hymn was sung, then the children were ushered out so that the adults could participate in what was referred to as communion. Our family had a strong interdenominational approach so we had attended churches of a variety of denominations and I had seen this sacrament administered in various ways. For some reason at my grandmother's church, children were excluded from this event, though the opportunity to get outside to play meant that I didn't really question the custom at the time.

This meal is known by many names across Christian denominations, Holy Communion, the Lord's Supper, Eucharist, Mass and the Breaking of Bread, among others, and the way it is administered along with the theology that accompanies it is similarly broad. The fascinating thing is that despite the differences, this meal is accepted almost universally across Christian expressions of worship. From an ornate cathedral where the sacrament is administered in a highly formal manner, to a handful of Aboriginal men and women sitting under a tree, drinking tea from a billy-can and eating a slab of damper, there is a reverence that resonates through this meal.

As I grew up I reflected on my experience at my grandmother's church and began to ask why children were excluded from something that was clearly significant to those adults who participated. Over time I began to understand that there was a concern that somehow children may fail to recognize the importance of the event and participate without due reverence. Their thinking was also based on a belief that communion was only for those people who had entered into faith in Christ through a 'born again' experience.

The apostle Paul wrote to the young church in the city of Corinth in Greece about their practice of incorporating the Lord's Supper in their worship services. It seems there was a problem that instead of taking a deliberate approach to this meal as an act of worship, they had turned it into a pot luck supper. The reverence was gone, and the focus was on filling their stomachs rather than honoring God through an act of worship. Paul's warning has been used by many wary pastors since who have been anxious to protect the meal from misuse.

> In the following directives I have no praise for you, for your meetings do more harm than good. In the first place, I hear that when you come together as a church, there are divisions among you, and to some extent I believe it. No doubt there have to be differences among you to show which of you have God's approval. So then, when you come together, it is not the Lord's Supper you eat, for when you are eating, some of you go ahead with your own private suppers. As a result, one person remains hungry and another gets drunk. Don't you have homes to eat and drink in? Or do you despise the church of God by humiliating those who have nothing? What shall I say to you? Shall I praise you? Certainly not in this matter!
>
> For I received from the Lord what I also passed on to you: The Lord Jesus, on the night he was betrayed, took bread, and when he had given thanks, he broke it and said, "This is my body, which is for you; do this in remembrance of me." In the same way, after supper he took the cup, saying, "This cup is the new covenant in my blood; do this, whenever you drink it, in remembrance of me." For whenever you eat this bread and drink this cup, you proclaim the Lord's death until he comes. So

then, whoever eats the bread or drinks the cup of the Lord in an unworthy manner will be guilty of sinning against the body and blood of the Lord. Everyone ought to examine themselves before they eat of the bread and drink from the cup. For those who eat and drink without discerning the body of Christ eat and drink judgment on themselves. That is why many among you are weak and sick, and a number of you have fallen asleep. But if we were more discerning with regard to ourselves, we would not come under such judgment. Nevertheless, when we are judged in this way by the Lord, we are being disciplined so that we will not be finally condemned with the world.

So then, my brothers and sisters, when you gather to eat, you should all eat together. Anyone who is hungry should eat something at home, so that when you meet together it may not result in judgment. And when I come I will give further directions. (1 Corinthians 11;17–34).

Theologian and author Scot McKnight explored this attempt to protect the sacrament, and recognizing the various denominational approaches, acknowledged their concerns came from a genuine place. In the long run, however, he expressed his personal preference for a more open approach.

> Matters like these are not decided by individuals, but by local churches and leaders. I would argue from the table fellowship of Jesus, which is where I think we need to begin any discussion of the Eucharist, that the table is open to all who want to focus their attention on Jesus' death and resurrection. My own view, within proper limits, is that this is not a meal so much in need of protection as it is a meal in need of missional extension. Come, we say, and see. Come and taste. Come find grace. If a person seeks for grace, this is where we want them to come. Why do we fling wide the doors? Because the Eucharist is a meal that offers atonement—with God, self, others, and the world.[1]

---

1. McKnight, *A Community Called Atonement*. 154

Asian-American Pentecostal theologian, Amos Yong also explored the various approaches to the sacrament and noted that the 18th century English cleric and theologian, John Wesley described the supper as a 'converting ordinance' and understood that the table was not closed to sinners seeking repentance. Yong's expressed view is that the hospitality of God is extended unconditionally and gratuitously to all, and "there are no barriers to Jesus' table except self-imposed ones." He said that in the earliest Christian communities, the breaking of bread occurred on a daily basis, from home to home, and in a dynamical process in and through which "outsiders" were initiated into the fellowship of believers.

> Following this model, might this notion of the "open table" be a bridge through which Christians can practice a form of liturgical hospitality in their encounter with those in other faiths? This does not require a formal enactment of the eucharistic sacrament; it only needs the informal but essentially hospitable practices of sharing meals with one another with gladness and generous hearts. It is precisely in such contexts that the many tongues of the Spirit may yet speak forth and reveal the presence of God to save the lost and transform the disciples of Jesus ever closer into his image.[2]

When God invited the Hebrew people to share in a simple meal as part of the process of release from slavery in Egypt, he initiated a custom that was intended to help people remember him for generations to come. As Jesus shared in that meal with his disciples, just as they did every year, he took bread, gave thanks and broke it, and gave it to them, saying, "This is my body given for you; do this in remembrance of me" (Luke 22:19). With these words, Jesus initiated a new way of eating together. He provided an opportunity for his followers to use ordinary everyday symbols, bread and wine, as a means of recalling his acts of death and resurrection, and reflecting on what it means to accept the invitation to eat at God's banquet table.

---

2. Yong. *Hospitality and the Other.* 131–136

A Stranger on the Road

How God the Maker, the consummate host, revealed himself to two travellers and in the process, the functions of host and guest were merged into one miraculous act of grace.

CLEOPAS AND HIS FRIEND had just had lunch and weren't really looking forward to the four-hour walk to their home in the township of Emmaus. The sun was beating down on them, the road was dusty, and there was a lot on their minds. As they walked they talked about all the events that had occurred in the last few days, particularly the news they had just received that morning.

They had been with a group of Jesus' disciples and the conversation had been intense. They were still bewildered at the events of the last few days. Their friend Jesus had gone through a terrible trial and had been put to death on a cross. It had all been very quick and their emotions were up and down. Some of the group were angry at what had happened, some seemed to have gone quiet and had withdrawn from the conversation, while others were arguing about all that had happened and were demanding answers.

Then this group of women turned up where they were meeting and told them they had gone to Jesus' tomb that morning and had found the stone had been rolled away from the front of the tomb. It seemed to be ridiculous but Peter had gone to check the tomb and he had come back and confirmed that the tomb was empty.

As they walked the two threw the stories around backwards and forwards. Maybe the women were just emotional and seeing things. But, no, Peter had confirmed it to be the case. Surely Peter wouldn't have been confused too? Maybe the rumor they had heard about Jesus' body being stolen was true. It seemed that the body wasn't in the tomb any more, but the women's message about angels saying Jesus was alive, seemed to be a bit far-fetched.

All the rumors and the conflicting stories were quite depressing, and as they walked their heads were down, scuffing the stones on the road, shoulders slumped, a sad sight for someone who may be walking along the road behind them. They weren't alone on the road. People used it all the time to get between Jerusalem, Emmaus and other towns along the way. So it wasn't surprising when they heard steps coming up behind them and found themselves joined by a fellow traveler.

They didn't look up. They were engrossed in their conversation. Confused, depressed, sad. They kept talking as they walked, dragging their feet a little, and the stranger who had come alongside them didn't say anything. He just listened.

Then he spoke. "What are you talking about?"

They stopped, stunned by his question. They may well have looked up at him, but didn't recognize him as Jesus.

"Are you the only one in Jerusalem who hasn't heard the things that have been going on?" they asked.

"What things?" he asked.

It didn't take much for them to start telling this stranger about Jesus. He had played such a significant role in their lives over the last few years that their thoughts and memories, along with their feelings, their hopes and dreams, just bubbled out. They told the stranger about the events of the last few days, how Jesus had been sent to trial, how he had been put to death on a Roman cross, and then the information they had received this morning about the tomb being empty.

A Stranger on the Road

The next thing they knew the stranger was explaining the Scriptures to them. There was nothing new in what he said. They regularly attended the synagogue and listened to the priests explaining Scripture. They had a firm belief in the Messiah and they had even suspected that Jesus himself may be the Messiah. But there was a freshness about what he was saying.

When they listened to the priests and elders in the synagogue each Sabbath they often seemed to be parroting off something they had memorized. They were genuine, honest men, but it did get a bit boring at times. But this stranger was speaking as if the message he was telling was something that came from his heart. Almost as if he had a personal knowledge of the Messiah himself.

The three of them were so engrossed in the conversation as they walked that they barely noticed the shadows were getting longer. The walk to Emmaus had never been so quick, but before they knew it they had arrived, and it looked like the stranger intended to walk on past the town. They urged him to stay with them and he accepted their offer. They were good hosts and quickly got some food together to make their guest feel at home, then they sat down at the table.

Before anything else could happen the stranger picked up one of the loaves they had put in the middle of the table. There was something familiar about his actions. Perhaps it was the way he held the loaf, and slowly began to break it in half. Perhaps it was the way he offered a prayer of thanks.

Suddenly they knew it was Jesus, sitting there in their home. He was their guest. They were all tired and hungry and Cleopas was anxious to look after this stranger well, yet in his action of breaking bread the stranger had become the host.

Then he was gone.

The pair looked at each other. They knew there was something about this person who had been walking with them all afternoon. It was as if their hearts were burning inside them, but they didn't get it. Now as they broke bread together Jesus had revealed himself to them and they knew that he was alive and all that he had said was true.

Come Eat With Me

They were tired and it was getting late, but the pair left the food on the table, rushed out of the house and ran back to Jerusalem to tell their friends what had happened. To their surprise, as they burst into the house where the disciples were gathered they found a very different situation to what they had left that morning.

"It's true," they were all shouting. "Jesus is alive and he's appeared to Simon."

Cleopas could hardly get a word in, but after the initial excitement the pair were able to share their own story of meeting Jesus on the road, and their experience of breaking bread.

The group was convinced. Jesus was truly alive.

You can read this story for yourself at Luke chapter 24

A Place of Healing

THE NORTH-WEST TOWN OF Roebourne where we lived in the early 90s, had a reputation for racism fueled by a number of high-profile incidents and the regular sight of drunken Aborigines lying on the footpath outside the ancient corrugated iron hotel in the town's main street. Nearly ten years before I took up the post as pastor of the Baptist Church, Roebourne had been the center of a major court hearing over the death of a sixteen-year-old Aboriginal boy, John Pat. Along with other Aboriginal teenagers, Pat was engaged in a fight with an Aboriginal police aide and three off-duty police officers outside the Roebourne Hotel. He was reportedly injured in the fight, but was arrested and taken to the lockup, where he died soon after.

The five police officers involved in the incident were tried on counts of manslaughter before a judge and an all-white jury and were all acquitted, attracting outcry from many sources.

As a bi-vocational pastor I needed to find alternative work to pay the bills and was successful in getting a position as education coordinator at the Roebourne Regional Prison, a few kilometers out of town. This large stone prison housed mainly Aboriginal prisoners, but isn't to be confused with the lock-up situated at the back of the police station where John Pat came to his untimely end. Nevertheless, I did get to visit that lock-up. When a small group of prisoners completed their training as Hiab crane operators, I accompanied them to the Roebourne police station to supervise the exam that would hopefully provide them with employment at the time of their release.

The dark back room of the police station where the exam was held was untidy and dusty. Pornographic magazines were scattered in the corner of the room, and cobwebs dangled from the ceiling. As I sat supervising the small group of prisoners I looked around at the walls that, if they could speak, would have had much to say about the day John Pat and his friends were discarded by the police and society at large.

The justice system, including the prison that was my workplace, was as far removed from a host environment as you could imagine. The dominant emotion was anger and it was rare to find respect. Control was firmly in the hands of the authorities.

But just down the road another influence was at work.

Despite Roebourne's dark reputation, the light of Christ shone brightly in a vibrant Apostolic church that positively impacted the lives of many Aboriginal people. The pastor and founder of the Pilbara Aboriginal Fellowship, David Stevens provided many opportunities for leadership to emerge from among the local Aboriginal Christians, and the influence of these Christians on the local community was significant. David Stevens may have never heard the term hosting when it comes to evangelism, but his style was definitely that of a host.

A veteran linguist and Bible translator with Aboriginal people in the Pilbara, Brian Geytenbeek reflected about events at an Easter convention some years later when the Christian leaders from Roebourne called a men's meeting to discuss some issues they had been facing for a few years. Brian very generously shared with me notes he had made in his diary.

> "David Stevens (their white Apostolic pastor) began by describing the trouble. For some time there had been lots of funerals in the Roebourne area. Everyone was grieving, church attendance fell away, week after week there were no testimonies about the Lord's dealings with people, either through His Word or through their

circumstances, no reports of answered prayer, no souls getting saved.

"As the elders had prayed about the state of the church they had come to realize that their Water Warlu (Water Snake – the Rainbow Serpent) was causing all these troubles; and as they studied the Bible they realized that their Water Snake is actually Satan, whom the Bible describes as the snake in the Garden of Eden in Genesis, and the great dragon in Revelation, and in various other places in between. And they had come to realize that if they make sure there is no sin in their lives, they do not need to fear him as they always have in the past, and they can fight against him and win using the Name of Jesus!

"This was a very liberating thought for them. They had come to realize that often they, and all their people, had not resisted him when they should have, simply because they had been afraid of what he might do to them or their families. But now they have discovered that if they are fully trusting the Father, and making Him "Number One" in their lives, they do not need to be afraid of the Rainbow Serpent!

"The elders decided that to defeat the snake's power over their people they had to wound his head. Where was that? Well, they figured that since his mouth is at Millstream, his head must be there too. (They did not want to actually see him close up, or they might see his eyes, and they knew that that would be very dangerous.) So they went to Millstream, the most sacred site in the whole of Yindjibarndi country, and held a prayer meeting up on a certain hill there, and claimed the victory over the Water Snake. And the number of sicknesses and deaths has dropped off since, and the church has picked up in heart and in numbers again."

In his diary, Brian Geytenbeek recalled the way an old Roebourne man had closed the meeting by praising David Stevens publicly for the way he had helped them over the years to find out what was in the Bible, without ever telling them what to do.

> "He never said to us, 'Look! Your culture's all wrong. You need to change to the whitefella culture.' If he had said that, we would have given up on him." Instead, whenever they had wanted to talk about aspects of culture, David had asked them what their culture taught about that particular aspect, and then shared with them whatever the Bible said about that same aspect. And then he would say to them, "Well, now you know what your culture says, and you know what the Bible says. What you do about it is between you and God. You go and talk to Him about it, and ask Him what he wants you to do."

David Stevens had put the individual at the center of the decision-making process. This is the action of a leader who is truly a host. Information is provided, boundaries are set, if necessary, and the individual is given the freedom to come to a decision. The outcome of that decision is then owned by the individual and long-term benefits emerge.

In contrast to this approach, some colonialist missionaries preached against local cultures, even banning their observance, in an effort to bring about change in the lives of their congregation. The upshot has been that either Christianity has been rejected outright, or people have adopted Christian beliefs and have maintained their cultural practices but kept them hidden from the missionaries. Conversion has been effected in the head but not in the heart.

In recent years the fear of proselytizing has been expressed widely. The dictionary definition (Merriam-Webster) of proselytize is to *induce someone to convert from one faith to another or to recruit a person to join another party or institutio*n. While religious proselytization has been condemned, it could be argued that the whole advertising industry is built on getting people to change their loyalty from one product to another. The real issue, is not the act of proselytizing but the way in which it is conducted. When a person changes their loyalty from one religion to another, from one political party to another or one brand of toothpaste to another the important issue is not that a change has occurred but how the change occurred. It is not appropriate for change to occur as a result of force or pressure, nor is it appropriate for deception or manipulation to occur in the process.

Yet deceit, manipulation, force and even violence have influenced some forms of Christian evangelism in the past. Evangelism in a host environment, however, can take on a very different form. The difference is the starting point.

When the starting point is the evangelist there is an assumption by that person that they are right and the person to whom they are speaking is wrong and needs to change. All my life in church I have been told that as Christians we are, in effect, receptacles of the truth and those who don't have the truth will be lost for eternity. The desire to save people from the fires of hell is a very genuine and noble desire but has led to the adoption of methods that give little thought to the credibility of the individual other than their eternal salvation.

A host evangelist may have the same beliefs about salvation, but will start with the individual. Their goal is to hear the story of where they come from and what they believe, honoring their identity. They will come to appreciate the family and cultural backgrounds that have influenced their beliefs, then as an equal will share their own beliefs and the reason for those beliefs.

In a place of mutual respect both parties may be equally convinced of the need of the other to join their respective faith but out of respect for each other, neither will misrepresent their case nor seek to force a decision to change.

It is in such a space that the freedom is given to the Holy Spirit to create change. The evangelist is no longer feeling under pressure to "convert" the other person but is able to let go, knowing that the person has all the information to make a decision to change and that the final decision is in the hands of God.

Henri Nouwen talks about developing inner space where the story can be received. Healing, he says, is the humble but also very demanding task of creating and offering a friendly empty space where strangers can reflect on their pain and suffering without fear, and find the confidence that makes them look for new ways right in the center of their confusion.

> "Healers are hosts who patiently and carefully listen to the story of the suffering strangers. Patients are guests who rediscover their selves by telling their story to the one who offers them a place to stay. In the telling of their stories, strangers befriend not only their host but also their own past."[1]

Nouwen says that reaching out to others without being receptive to them is more harmful than helpful and easily leads to manipulation and even to violence, violence in thoughts, words and actions. This was evident in the words of the Aboriginal elder who said that they would have rejected Christianity if it had been presented without first hearing the stories of their culture.

"Really honest receptivity means inviting the stranger into our world on his or her own terms, not on ours," Nouwen says. "When we say, 'you can be my guest if you believe what I believe, think the way I think and behave as I do,' we offer love under a condition or for a price. This leads only to exploitation, making hospitality into a business."

Immediately, I can hear people arguing that a Christian should speak the truth clearly if they are to be obedient to the commandments of Christ to preach the Gospel. We are often faced with the dilemma of speaking out the Gospel as opposed to living the Gospel and the words of Francis of Assisi are often quoted: "Preach the Gospel at all times, and when necessary, use words."

Nouwen addresses this by talking about the boundaries that need to be set in establishing that welcoming space. He describes an empty house that is made available to strangers and says that it would not be hospitable to make such a space available, then to allow the strangers to use it in any way they want. The guest, he says would not lose their fears in an empty house, but would become anxious and suspicious of noises coming from the attic

---

1. Nouwen. *Reaching Out.*

or the cellar. Instead, we can enter into communication when our own life choices, attitudes and viewpoints offer the boundaries that challenge strangers to become aware of their own position and to explore it critically.

> "As a reaction to a very aggressive, manipulative and often degrading type of evangelization, we sometimes have become hesitant to make our own religious convictions known, thereby losing our sense of witness. Although at times it seems better to deepen our own commitments than to evangelize others, it belongs to the core of Christian spirituality to reach out to the other with good news and to speak without embarrassment about what we have heard and . . . seen with our own eyes . . . watched and touched with our hands' (1John1:1)"[2]

After Jesus' resurrection, Peter and the other disciples met Jesus on the beach one day, and Jesus cooked them breakfast at the conclusion of a hard night's fishing. He then took the opportunity to challenge Peter to take the next step in his growth as a disciple of Jesus. For Peter, that challenge would mean that he would need to translate all that he had *seen with his own eyes, watched and touched with his hands* into real life care for others. Peter was about to learn what it meant to be both host and guest in his interactions with both friends and strangers.

---

2. Nouwen. *Reaching Out*

Breakfast on the Beach

How God the Maker, the consummate host, initiated a simple beach breakfast to call on a new level of commitment from one of his dearly-loved followers.

THE WATER FELT GOOD as it lapped at the shores of the lake and splashed over John's feet, then slurried back to where it had come. He shivered slightly, bracing himself for the next wave to make its way up to the beach. It was dark and cold, and John's shoulders were slumped. The cool water on his feet was the only thing that seemed to ease the tension he felt in his body.

The days since Jesus had come back to life had been difficult for John and the rest of Jesus' disciples. They had been filled with a range of emotions as memories flooded back of the terrible days leading up to his death. He still had flashbacks of those events, and particularly that dreadful evening at Golgotha when he witnessed Jesus' death. Then beyond all expectations, Jesus had come back to life and they had spent glorious days together remembering the past and being reassured that their beloved friend really was alive.

But things were different now. One moment Jesus would be with them and it was as if he'd never gone; then there were times like this when a deep sadness overwhelmed him. Suddenly out of the darkness, a voice called out and John looked up, unaware that he had been walking slower and slower. His friends were now out of sight, walking somewhere in front of him along the shore of

Lake Galilee, but he looked towards the spot where he could hear the voice.

"What's up?" he called back.

"We're going fishing."

He knew Peter's voice and he knew that Peter was feeling the same as him, and had probably decided that there was no better way to break out of this emotional whirlpool than to get back into the boat.

"Wait for me," John called as he began jogging towards the voices that now exuded a sense of excitement. Within a short time the six men were in the boat and, like a machine, working together in unity to get the boat where they wanted it and drop the nets into the water . They weren't far from shore, but it was one of their favourite spots and it had never failed them before.

Dawn was beginning to throw its colours into the eastern sky when the six men aboard the boat heard a voice calling from shore. It was Jesus.

"Caught anything?" Jesus called out.

They were cold and tired, frustrated. They knew this spot well, but for the first time they could recall, they hadn't been able to get a single fish all night. Thomas snapped back: "Not a thing!"

"Try throwing your net on the other side and you'll do better," Jesus called out of the darkness.

"The fishermen mumbled under their breath for a moment. We're the fishermen here. What would he know? Then Peter said, "it's worth a try. Come on guys. Last chance!"

John was tired as well, but he admired Peter's stamina and his willingness to follow the advice of his master. They all seemed to gain some new strength as John pulled his weight with the others in throwing the net onto the other side of the boat. Without warning there was a splash in the distance, then another and before long the water was churning as a massive school of fish headed past the boat and into the waiting nets. All their tiredness was gone as six burly fishermen began yelling out at once like schoolboys. As they pulled the net in they were overwhelmed at their early morning catch.

Fortunately, they weren't far from shore so it didn't take long to get back and pull their boat up on the beach. It was just starting to get light and they could see Jesus kneeling down in front of a small fire. He was baking some bread on the coals and as they came towards him, he asked them to bring some of their fish. After a cold and unproductive night, there was nothing better than sitting around a fire on the beach eating breakfast of fish and bread.

John pulled himself a little closer to the fire as he tucked into the piece of fish Jesus had handed him. He remembered something like this happening before. His mind went back to the time when Jesus had been teaching a great crowd of people on the hillside not far from where they were now. All they had was a few pieces of fish and some bread rolls, but somehow Jesus had fed all those people. Once again he was hosting his friends to a meal. Yet it was such a simple occasion. A fire, some bread he had made himself, and some fish they wouldn't have had if it hadn't been for Jesus' advice.

A feed had restored the fishermen and as they laughed and recalled the events of the night, they didn't notice that Jesus and Peter had quietly slipped away. John became aware of their absence and quietly got up to follow them. He took advantage of the dawn shadows and stayed far enough away so he couldn't be seen, but he could hear enough of the conversation between Jesus and Peter to know that this would be a turning point for Peter.

He could see that Peter was getting frustrated at Jesus' questioning, but Jesus remained firm. Through the early morning mist John heard Jesus saying to Peter, "Feed my sheep." It seemed a strange statement, but John thought for a moment of the breakfast he had just eaten. Jesus had hosted his beloved friends to a simple meal of bread and fish after a frustrating night, now he was passing on the role of host to Peter.

For some reason, John had a sense that Jesus had given his friend Peter a very special responsibility. He didn't really understand the words, 'feed my sheep', but he knew that it involved caring for those people Jesus loved in a manner that would reflect the grace that Jesus had bestowed on him. Deep down, John also knew that the challenge would bring about a dramatic change in Peter's life in the days and months to come.

You can read this story for yourself at John chapter 21

A Bowl of Rice

I LOOKED AROUND THE room of the drab Housing Commission house and there wasn't a skerrick of furniture to be seen other than the basics that were built into the house, a gas stove, kitchen cupboards and a well-used laminex-coated bench. We were sitting on the floor in the middle of the lounge room, myself and a group of young Iraqi men. In front of us on the floor was a huge bowl of rice the men had quickly prepared.

The men, refugees from war-torn Iraq, had arrived on the west coast of Australia some months earlier on board a rickety Indonesian fishing boat and were promptly incarcerated in an immigration detention center. During their time there, one of the men, Saeed, had converted to Christianity as a result of visits by an elderly Christian lady who had made it her duty to visit the center on a regular basis. When she had heard that Saeed and his friends had been released and had found abattoir work in the town where I lived she had contacted me and asked me to visit.

I was overwhelmed at the welcome I received when I went to visit, and the way in which they openly shared their stories. Most of them were professional men who had left their wives and families in search of a new life with the intention of one day bringing their families to Australia to join them. They had suffered great trauma under the Iraqi regime, and had faced possible death by choosing to sail to Australia in a craft that was probably not suited to the types of seas they would encounter.

A Bowl of Rice

There was something unexpected about this situation: A white Christian pastor in a small Western Australian town being hosted by a group of Iraqi refugees, mostly Muslim. As we sat on the floor around that bowl of rice, eating with our fingers, the differences in religion, race and culture seemed to fade away. A shared meal brought us together and made it possible to hear each other's stories and build a relationship based on respect and trust.

Graham Hill of the *Global Church Project* says that the church's hospitality is a participation in the mission of God and an expression of its hopeful expectation.

> A hospitable spirituality welcomes "unexpected guests" at God's multicultural banquet table. It witnesses to Jesus in our life together and toward the world. We are hospitable because God is hospitable.[1]

It is inevitable that we will hold certain prejudices based on our upbringing, the cultural preferences that are common to the society or community in which we have grown up, and even the way we have been taught to understand our own religious preferences. Acting differently to people of other cultures or religions often requires a radical change of thinking, and our understanding of Jesus is critical to this change. Hill expanded on this by saying:

> The church's hospitality is a participation in the mission of God and an expression of its hopeful expectation. Hospitality gives us a taste of that which is to come. We are welcoming the stranger and neighbor to God's banquet table. This is a table where all socio-cultures, ethnicities, languages, genders and people groups are welcome. They are welcome to take part in the hospitality of God. An inclusive church embodies this hospitality. More broadly, Jesus Christ reveals this hospitality wherever his inaugurated kingdom is present.[2]

Most of my life I've heard teaching in church that Christianity was somehow exclusive; that when a person is aligned with

---

1. Hill, *GlobalChurch*. 1555–1556
2. Hill. *GlobalChurch*. 1555–1556

God by faith in Christ, they had a responsibility to withdraw from those who may somehow "taint" their faith. Paul's injunction to the Corinthian church: "Come out from them and be separate, says the Lord" was drummed into young converts to the point that many Christians developed a fortress mentality and over time cut themselves off from anyone who wasn't the same as them.

What we never heard when Paul was quoted, was that this was only part of the story. In context the verse reads like this: *What agreement is there between the temple of God and idols? For we are the temple of the living God. As God has said, "I will live with them and walk among them, and I will be their God, and they will be my people." Therefore, "Come out from them and be separate, says the Lord. Touch no unclean thing, and I will receive you"* (Second Corinthians 6:16, 17).

Paul was speaking here about the strong bond that was established between God and his people and that as a result of this bond, a natural separation would occur from anything that was incompatible with this relationship. This was much the same as a married couple who would commit to each other and separate themselves from carrying on other relationships outside of their marriage. Such a commitment to the marriage relationship does not preclude genuine platonic friendships, but recognizes the sanctity and uniqueness of that relationship. The interesting thing about this instruction from Paul is the way he referred to the temple and God's presence among his people.

The presence of God, and the promise that he would *live with them and walk among them . . .* was at the heart of the covenant that God made with his people. This promise of being present with his people requires a similar response from his people as they consider their place in the world. Amos Yong, in his book *Hospitality and the Other: Pentecost, Christian Practices, and the Neighbor*, claims that the Christian mission is nothing more or less than our participation in the hospitality of God. He says God is not only the principal missionary but also the host of all creation who invites the world to "God's banquet of salvation." This, he claims, means that there is an important responsibility to the other.

> Remembering that hospitality involves a set of relationships between guests and hosts, and that Christian mission inevitably involves us as both guests and hosts, we must recognize that our embracing strangers of other faiths involves them also doing the same. Hence, our desire for them to embrace our beliefs and enter into our practices must be matched by our willingness to do the same.[3]

For some, particularly those who may have called on us to "come out from among them," this causes concern that such embracing of strangers will compromise our faith. Yong argues that this is not the case but that Christian mission should be conducted from the vantage point of being guests of those of other faiths, and as we do that we not only defer to our hosts, but we also receive from them as aliens in a strange land. He claims this is not a "blurry syncretism," but a deepening of the home tradition as enriched by the gift of others. Yong says differences are not swallowed by what he calls the home-dwelling, but that dwelling is enlarged and enriched through the extending of frontiers.

> Hence, the Christian mission involves the reconciliation of aliens and strangers (ourselves) to God, and our making available this reconciliation to other aliens and strangers by becoming reconciled to them. The missio Dei is in this sense a "stranger-centered" theology that follows in the footsteps of Jesus: the Son of God became a stranger, coming into a far country, even to the point of death. Here, Christian mission is the embodiment of divine hospitality that loves strangers (philoxenia), to the point of giving up our lives on behalf of others as to be reconciled to them, that they might in turn be reconciled to God.[4]

As I sat on the floor of an old housing commission house, eating rice with a group of Iraqi men, mostly Muslim, my faith was enriched, and my eyes were opened to the privilege of being both

---

3. Yong. *Hospitality and the Other.* 131–136
4. Yong. *Hospitality and the Other.* 131–136

host and guest in the presence of people of other faiths and cultures. It was through the presence of God that, we, together could begin to understand what it meant to be reconciled to God.

The Dream That Changed the World

How God the Maker, the consummate host, intervened in the life of two men and radically changed their way of thinking about him and those around them.

LUKE WAS DELIGHTED THAT Peter had asked to meet him. They had been mates for years, but in recent times hadn't had much time to get together. They were sitting together not far from the lake where Peter plied his trade as a fisherman, but clearly he had asked to meet Luke for a more pressing reason than to talk about fishing. Even before Luke could pick up his pen, Peter was excitedly telling him about a dream that he had.

"Wait, wait," Luke interrupted. "Let's go back to the beginning. If you want me to write this down, I need to get the story clear right from the beginning."

"Sorry," Peter said, pausing for a moment. "It's just been so exciting."

Luke was a doctor and was the sort that you would be happy to trust your life with if the need came for some serious surgery. He was a person who was serious, meticulous and fastidious. He was also like that in his writing, and that was why Peter wanted him to record the details of his dream and the events that occurred later. Peter was aware that Luke had been carefully recording events relating to their experiences with Jesus and things that had been happening since Jesus had gone away.

"So where were you when all this happened," Luke asked, ready to start recording what Peter was about to tell him.

"I'd gone up on the roof of the house to pray," he started. "I was starving and I had asked my wife to organise some lunch. The next thing, I go to sleep and start dreaming about food."

"I've told you before about eating too much before bedtime. It doesn't just give you indigestion, but obviously makes you dream as well!"

"I hadn't even eaten at that stage," Peter said. "But you wouldn't believe it, I saw this kind of sheet coming out of heaven, held by its four corners, and it was filled with all these animals that our religion says you can't eat. There were pigs and camels, and lizards, and ravens and eagles and owls. It's all forbidden. All my life I've been told we can't eat animals that have cloven hoofs or chew the cud. I remember my rabbi telling me as a kid that these animals are an abomination to eat.

"You're right," Luke added. "It's always been accepted as part of our religion. So what happened?"

"Well, I heard this voice, and it said 'get up Peter, kill and eat.'"

"What did you do? You wouldn't eat any of those animals would you—even in your dreams?" Luke asked.

"That's exactly what I thought. I said to the voice, 'I've never eaten anything unclean or impure'. You know me, Luke. I've always been fussy about that. I just couldn't bring myself to eat any of those animals."

"So what happened next?" Luke asked.

"Well the voice said: 'Do not call anything impure that God has made clean.'"

"Wow, what do you think that meant?"

"I don't know, but the voice asked me three times to get up and kill and eat these unclean animals, and each time it told me not to call anything impure that God has made clean. Then, I woke up."

The Dream That Changed the World

"That's one weird dream, Peter," Luke said. "Thanks for telling me about it; I've written it all down carefully. Have you any idea what it was all about?"

"That's not the end of the story," Peter interjected. There's more. I'm sitting there rubbing my eyes and I hear a disturbance downstairs, and I had this strong sense that I needed to go downstairs and do something special. I'm sure it was the Holy Spirit prompting me. So I headed downstairs and there's a couple of Roman soldiers who said they had been sent by their officer and he wanted to see Peter."

"What did they say?" Luke asked.

Well they said, 'we have come from Cornelius the centurion. He is a righteous and God-fearing man, who is respected by all the Jewish people. A holy angel told him to ask you to come to his house so that he could hear what you have to say.' It turns out a few days earlier Cornelius had had a dream as well and he had been told to look me up."

"So what's this all got to do with your dream?" Luke asked.

"That's the interesting thing, Peter replied. Before I had that dream, I wouldn't be seen walking along the road with a couple of Roman soldiers, you wouldn't have caught me dead in the home of a Roman centurion, and I certainly wouldn't have thought it possible that a Roman centurion could be baptized into the name of Jesus Christ."

"Baptized. What are you talking about?" Luke asked.

"Well, I went to Cornelius' home with his soldiers, and it turned out I got on quite well with them. Then I met Cornelius and we had a great time together. Despite being a Roman centurion, he was drinking in everything I told him about Jesus. I suddenly realized that God doesn't show favoritism, that he accepts from every nation those who fear him and do what is right. We sat there and I shared with him the good news about Jesus and before I left that day, Cornelius and everyone who was in the room were baptized.

Luke paused from writing and said: "You know, Peter, that was an amazing story. God has taught you an incredibly important truth, and I want to congratulate you for listening to the voice of God and taking notice of his message."

As Peter and Luke sat and went over the story again and again, they became overwhelmed at the significance of what Peter had experienced. Before that they were both convinced that only the Jews had the right to be accepted by God, but as they talked they suddenly realized that even before Peter had his dream, Jesus had been preparing them for this time. As the pair looked out over the lake they were unaware of the changes that would occur as a result of Peter's dream.

You can read this story for yourself at Acts chapter 10

The Water of Life

I REMEMBER AT SCHOOL being taught about how to write a story. There should always be a beginning and an end and the story should include the elements of characters, the setting, the plot, the conflict, and the resolution. Readers of the Bible often assume that it is simply a collection of different writings from different authors and different places, with little to connect the dots. Alternatively, some will see the Bible as something like a jar of sweets consisting of different shapes and colors and tastes. Depending on your particular need or taste at that time, you can dip into the jar and find a verse of Scripture, that will address your need and provide encouragement or guidance.

However, I prefer to think of the Bible as a story, a grand story, that has a beginning and an end and includes an amazing collection of characters, a setting, a gripping plot, a herculean conflict and a resolution. Scot McKnight in *The Blue Parakeet: Rethinking How You Read the Bible* describes the many stories within the Bible as wiki-stories of the main story. Sometimes, he says, one author will pick up the story of another author, and sometimes an author will tell a new version of an old story. But each of these wiki-stories are held together by the Story with a capital S.

> If we are invited to love God by reading the Bible as God's communication with us, then a relational approach to the Bible invites us to listen to God (the person) speak in the Bible and to engage God as we listen. The relational approach knows the Bible is filled with

wiki-stories—timely stories of the Story by human authors. But our approach believes the Bible is more than human wiki-stories. These authors are divinely guided so that their wiki-stories tell God's story. If we once admit this, we are summoned to stand in front of the Bible as those listening to God's story.[1]

There are many aspects to the story, but in this book, I have looked at the way the plot has been influenced by an invitation to eat at God's table, and how through the process of history, that plot has developed. We have discovered that the Bible starts with an amazing picture of God's hospitality in the garden, and it ends in a similar way with what is described as the marriage supper of the Lamb.

From the time Adam and Eve decided to rebel against God's hospitality, the Bible tells the story of how God proceeded to restore that relationship. It leads us through the establishment of Israel and all the ups and downs of that journey; it leads us to the coming of Jesus and his act of redemption achieved through his death and resurrection; it provides wisdom for the followers of Jesus as they band together in a movement that developed the name "church"; and it brings us, finally, to the time when Jesus is re-united with that church as his pure bride.

The Story begins in a garden where everything is perfect and there are all kinds of food available to the first people. The final book of the Bible, the Revelation of St John, shows how the beauty of Eden will be restored. The story concludes with another astounding act of hospitality, the marriage feast of the lamb when the creator and the created are brought together as one. Finally, the host gives his invitation: "The Spirit and the bride say, 'Come!' And let the one who hears say, 'Come!' Let the one who is thirsty come; and let the one who wishes take the free gift of the water of life."

A sub-plot through this grand story is the way in which those who accept the invitation to eat with their Maker are presented with some responsibilities. These include the need to share their story with others, to share the grace they have received with

---

1. McKnight. *The Blue Parakeet*. 88–89

others, and to act in ways that reflect the kind of example that has been set for them. Furthermore, that grace-sharing impacts not only our beliefs, but more significantly, affects our behaviors. The act of hospitality becomes a part of our lifestyle and we are challenged about the types of people to whom we offer that hospitality. Christine Pohl describes this as a habit of hospitality.

> A habit of hospitality is fundamental to our identity as Christians. Our primary call is to live out the gospel; a life-style of hospitality is part of that call. For some of us, there will be a more particular call to a deliberate and focused expression of hospitality, but for all of us hospitality is essential to who we are as followers of Jesus.[2]

As we accept the invitation to sit at the table of our Maker we are given the privilege of listening to the great stories of the faith, and appreciating the way in which history speaks of God's act of redemption. We are to enjoy the banquet of good things that come from sharing his table; good things like love, joy, peace, grace, hope, forgiveness, and the list goes on. But as we sit at the table we experience the discomfort of knowing that eating at that table requires a response that may take us out of our comfort zone.

In the final book of the Bible, John the Revelator, as he was described in 1930 by American gospel-blues musician, Blind Willie Johnson, saw into the future and in some way experienced the conclusion to the Grand Story. He recognized that in the midst of the conflict that had been woven through that story, a resolution was being achieved and would one day come to fruition. As he sat on the island of Patmos, exiled as a result of the persecution being carried out by the Roman emperor Domitian, John began to understand that a time would come when the beauty of Eden would be restored and that a new world would emerge.

As John put quill to papyrus to record his experiences and thoughts, the challenge that came from his visions was not lost.

2. Pohl. *Making Room*. 1996–1997

Come Eat With Me

Those who were privileged to eat with their Maker had been given a mission and the impact of the invitation to participate in that mission could not be ignored.

The Final Banquet

How God the Maker, the consummate host, celebrated the ultimate feast with his bride.

JOHN EASED HIMSELF ONTO a large rock where he could sit and look out to sea. In front of him the water glistened, only broken by small islands reaching out of the azure water. Behind him rugged hills towered above the small protected beach. The Greek island of Patmos was only a day's boat trip from Ephesus where John had been leading the local church.

His commitment to preach the Gospel of Jesus had led to the authorities hunting him down and ultimately shipping him out to Patmos. He wasn't alone on the island, but he was lonely, separated from friends and family. John gazed out to sea. The cool breeze blew in from the Aegean Sea and ruffled his white hair and beard. He was feeling his age lately, but his faith in Jesus was sustaining him. He wondered whether he would live long enough to make it back to Ephesus or if he would end his days on this lonely Greek island.

John reflected on his time on Patmos and the depth of spiritual experience he had been going through. Some recent earthquakes had shaken the island and sunsets were blood-red as a result of volcanoes erupting on nearby islands. A few nights ago as he sat in the mouth of his cave high up on the craggy island he imagined the molten lava running down the side of the mountain and hissing as it reached the water below. Lightning pierced the darkness and he could hear the massive waves crashing onto the shore, the effects of the earthquakes that had shaken his island home. As the thunder rolled across the stormy ocean and lightning flashed from one horizon to another he saw angels coming down from heaven.

Throughout the night the thunder roared as the volcano spewed lava into the ocean. Burning sulphur bubbled on the surface of the ocean and horrific beasts rose up and devoured the heavy rain clouds that rolled ferociously across the seascape, sometimes touching the waves that rose up towards the heavens. Lightning split the heavens open, revealing angels, dragons and mighty warriors on horseback.

In the daylight the world looked different but the impact of that night was still with him. He shivered as the cool sea breeze blew across his skin that was now perspiring profusely as he thought back on that experience. In generations to come he would become known as John the Revelator but for now he knew that he had to quickly get someone to help him write down his experiences.

Then almost without realizing the change, John felt at peace. He had seen the lamb appear in the midst of the terrible vision that night and now he could sense the presence of the lamb again. The storms had passed and the ocean was still, glistening under a cloudless sky. The water sparkled as the sun played with the gentle wavelets that seemed unaware of the ferocious storms a few nights earlier, and out of the center of the sun a figure appeared to John that looked like a bride dressed all in white.

His mind went back to a story that Jesus had told him and the other disciples about the coming of the bridegroom. It was about ten young women who were waiting for the bridegroom. Five of them were prepared for the event while the other five had not taken the time to get enough oil for their lamps. Although they had been waiting for a while, when the shout went out at midnight that the bridegroom was coming they realized they didn't have enough oil for their lamps and had to go searching for a re-fill. In the meantime, the bridegroom arrived and the five missed the opportunity to go to the banquet.

The Final Banquet

Now as John sat on the pebble beach at Patmos, looking across the Aegean Sea, the clouds came down lower, the sea disappeared and a great city descended from the clouds and he saw it was the bride, dressed in white. She shone and glistened like pure gemstones and John knew he was in the presence of the consummate host who had invited him to join him for the final great wedding banquet.

All of creation had been preparing for this time. The consummate host had created the beautiful garden and invited Adam and Eve to come and dine with him. When they and their children squandered the opportunity, he had prepared another beautiful feast of milk and wild honey and invited his people to a promised land where they could enjoy his presence at the table. Other opportunities arose through history where people were invited to dine with the consummate host and despite their repeated rejections, he ultimately gave up his role as host to become the guest himself. He took the last seat at the table to make room for the poor, the cripple, the blind and the lame. He scoured the country lanes and the back streets to invite people to join him and he died a pauper's death.

Now as John watched this shining city, this glorious bride, come down from heaven he understood the reason that down through time, humanity had been invited to dine with the consummate host. Although people had rejected the invitation more often than they had accepted it, the invitation was not revoked and bit by bit, over the centuries, the recipients of the invitation, the church of Jesus Christ, had been prepared for this time when the bridegroom would receive his bride at the final great wedding supper.

As the vision slowly faded and John found himself sitting on the pebble beach at Patmos he reflected on his own role as pastor of the church in Ephesus and how he had been sent as an exile to this rocky, desolate island because of his faithfulness to his Lord. The church was still being prepared and at times the preparation was painful. Yet there was a purpose and in his vision, John had the privilege of seeing the final great supper.

Come Eat With Me

If he had the chance to get back to Ephesus he would use the last few years of his life to remind the church that they were part of a plan that started before creation and would continue until completion. He would remind his dear brothers and sisters that they were the recipients of an amazing invitation and that unlike many of their forebears it would be crazy to ignore the invitation or to squander the opportunity to dine with the consummate host and enjoy eating at his table.

He would also remind them that the time had come for those who accepted the invitation to dine with their host to become hosts themselves. He would urge them to go out into the streets and country lanes, and extend his invitation to those who were far away and were not even aware that a great banquet had been prepared.

A gentle breeze wafted in from the ocean. The clouds were lifting and the sun's rays sparkled on the waves. His job was not complete. Until that last great banquet, the church could no longer act as guests expecting the best place to be set at the table for them. There was work to be done; a banquet to prepare.

You can read this for yourself in the book of Revelation

In the Presence of My Enemies

THE ROAD STRETCHED OUT in front of me like a strip of liquorice, disappearing into the distance unbroken. Occasionally a flash of light in the distance indicated that a road train or another car were approaching from the opposite direction I was travelling. The approaching vehicle provided some distraction from the long drive. Then it was gone. Over many years of travelling in the north west of Western Australia I became familiar with the road between Perth and Geraldton, a 433km ribbon of bitumen bounded on both sides by bushland apart from an occasional roadhouse and a few tiny hamlets.

Low scrub and scraggly trees reached out on either side of the road as far as the eye could see. The presence of human activity rarely interrupted the view apart from occasional signs along the road alerting drivers to the presence of a roadhouse another hundred or two kilometers farther up the road. The road didn't change. The scenery didn't change. So when something different appeared it was a welcome distraction, and I pulled the car over to the side of the road.

Every so often, a bushfire would ravish the countryside and the change in scenery was noticeable. Bushfires weren't uncommon and before Europeans came to Australia, the Aboriginal inhabitants used fire to manage the land and to ensure a plentiful food supply. Many native plants and animals developed special characteristics that enabled them to survive during and after a fire and some native plants required fire to regenerate or to release their seeds.

A bushfire had gone through this area a month or two earlier. The bushland that had been evident kilometer after kilometer was now replaced by a spot that had been left black and denuded by a fierce bushfire a month or two earlier. The charred landscape appeared devoid of life as I stepped from my car.

As I walked through an area that had once been covered in heavy undergrowth and dense bush I was confronted by the devastating effects of a fire that had left trees and bushes, and even the sand beneath my feet, black and lifeless. But as I looked closer it was clear that lifeless was not the correct word to describe this place.

Tiny green shoots were breaking through the dry sand at my feet, and splashes of bright green contrasted with the blackness of burnt tree trunks as fresh shoots pushed aside charcoal and stretched towards the sunlight. Leaves were forming like fresh symbols of life in a deathly environment.

It's sad that there are some passages of Scripture that only get to see the sunlight in times of death. I was taking a funeral one day and had chosen to read Psalm 23. But as I stood in the chapel of the funeral home reading the words of this Psalm something hit me that I hadn't noticed previously. It went like this:

> Even though I walk through the darkest valley, I will fear no evil, for you are with me; your rod and your staff, they comfort me. You prepare a table before me in the presence of my enemies. You anoint my head with oil; my cup overflows. Surely your goodness and love will follow me all the days of my life, and I will dwell in the house of the Lord forever.

You prepare a table for me. There it was again. God the Maker, the consummate host, had prepared a table for me. Not just a table in a new land where I would be protected from evil, but a table in the presence of my enemies. Whatever dark valley I would go through, the fresh green shoots of God's love and grace would continue to push through. No matter how burnt or decimated my

In the Presence of My Enemies

habitat had become there was a table where I would be welcome, safe and refreshed.

Even in the presence of enemies the table of grace will be prepared for me. Whether those enemies are people who bring fear and anguish to my life, or those enemies of death, disease, unemployment, loss, or poverty that bang angrily at the windows of my life, the table is still spread for me.

It is a table of life. A table that welcomes me when I don't feel welcome in other situations. A table that offers hope and refreshment. It is a table that groans with the weight of fresh fruit, and delicious food. The contrast between the bright colours of the food and the blackness of the scenery around me is unbelievable.

On this table is the bread and wine that speaks of the overwhelming grace of One who was prepared to go through the darkest valley on my behalf. It is the table where Jesus sits with a ragtag group of disciples, one of whom had just revealed his location to enemy soldiers in exchange for financial reward. It is the table where prostitutes and tax collectors sit, along with religious leaders who were finding opportunity to accuse Jesus of blasphemy. It is the table where I feel at home, yet at the same time in awe of the one who has offered me this momentous invitation.

And while I long to withdraw from this blackened place where my enemies hover in the shadows, I am drawn to this incredible table that has been set for me. Here in the presence of my enemies I experience forgiveness as I eat of the bread and drink of the wine; I can feel the oil of joy running down my head . . . and I know that I am at home.

What's next? If this book has prompted some thoughts in your own mind about your relationship with God, don't just put the book on the shelf and leave it there. Begin to read the Bible for yourself and discover more about the consummate host and what it means to eat at his table.

Find a church where you have the freedom to explore the challenges of Scripture, and find an individual or small group with whom you can be accountable to as you seek to grow closer in your relationship with God.

As you come across obstacles or challenges, remember those people like the widow of Zarephath, Abraham, the two spies Caleb and Joshua, Zacchaeus, Peter and John, who didn't give up despite all the opposition they received. You have received an amazing invitation from the maker of the universe.

Receive that invitation, reply to the RSVP, and join the banquet.

> Here I am! I stand at the door and knock. If anyone hears my voice and opens the door, I will come in and eat with that person, and they with me. Revelation 3:20

Bibliography

Brown, Cavan. *Pilgrim Through This Barren Land*. Albatross 1991.
Cowman, L.B. and Reimann, J. *Streams in the Desert*, Zondervan, 1997
DeBorst, Ruth Padilla. Unexpected Guests at God's Banquet Table: Gospel in Mission and Culture," *Evangelical Review of Theology*. 33, no. 1. 2009.
Frost, Michael. *Surprise the World: The Five Habits of Highly Missional People*. NavPress. 2015
Hill, Graham. *GlobalChurch: Reshaping Our Conversations, Renewing Our Mission, Revitalizing Our Churches*. InterVarsity Press. 2018
Hirsch, Alan and Ford, Lance. *Right Here, Right Now*. Grand Rapids, MI: Baker, 2011
McKergow, Mark; Bailey, Helen. *Host*, Solutions 2014
McKnight, Scot. *A Community Called Atonement: Living Theology*. Abingdon 2007
McKnight, Scot. *The Blue Parakeet: Rethinking How You Read the Bible*. Zondervan 2008
Meyer, Ben F. *The Aims of Jesus*. London: SCM 1979
Nouwen, Henri. *Reaching Out: The Three Movements of the Spiritual Life*, Doubleday 1975
Pohl. Christine D. *Making Room: Recovering Hospitality As a Christian Tradition*, Eerdmans 1999
Stott, John R. W. *Basic Christianity*. Inter-Varsity, 1958
Willard, Dallas. *Renewing the Christian Mind: Essays, Interviews, and Talks*. HarperCollins. 2016
Wright N.T. http://ntwrightpage.com/2016/03/30/the-ear-of-the-servant-the-tongue-of-the-teacher/
Yong, Amos. *Hospitality and the Other: Pentecost, Christian Practices, and the Neighbor* . Faith Meets Faith Series. Orbis 2008

www.ingramcontent.com/pod-product-compliance
Lightning Source LLC
Chambersburg PA
CBHW071439160426
43195CB00013B/1962